Primary Mistake

Susan –

Primary Mistake

How the Washington Republican Establishment
Lost Everything in 2006 (and Sabotaged My
Senatorial Campaign)

Thanks So much

STEVE LAFFEY

For you Help!

Steve

SENTINEL

SENTINEL
Published by the Penguin Group
Penguin Group (USA) Inc., 375 Hudson Street, New York, New York 10014, U.S.A.
Penguin Group (Canada), 90 Eglinton Avenue East, Suite 700,
Toronto, Ontario, Canada M4P 2Y3 (a division of Pearson Penguin Canada Inc.)
Penguin Books Ltd, 80 Strand, London WC2R 0RL, England
Penguin Ireland, 25 St. Stephen's Green, Dublin 2, Ireland
(a division of Penguin Books Ltd.)
Penguin Books Australia Ltd, 250 Camberwell Road, Camberwell,
Victoria 3124, Australia (a division of Pearson Australia Group Pty Ltd)
Penguin Books India Pvt Ltd, 11 Community Centre, Panchsheel Park,
New Delhi - 110 017, India
Penguin Group (NZ), 67 Apollo Drive, Rosedale, North Shore 0745,
Auckland, New Zealand (a division of Pearson New Zealand Ltd.)
Penguin Books (South Africa) (Pty) Ltd, 24 Sturdee Avenue,
Rosebank, Johannesburg 2196, South Africa

Penguin Books Ltd, Registered Offices:
80 Strand, London WC2R 0RL, England

First published in 2007 by Sentinel,
a member of Penguin Group (USA) Inc.

10 9 8 7 6 5 4 3 2 1

LIBRARY OF CONGRESS CATALOGING-IN-PUBLICATION DATA
Laffey, Steve.
    Primary mistake : how the Washington Republican Establishment lost everything in
2006 (and sabotaged my senatorial campaign) Steve Laffey
    p.   cm.
Includes bibliographical references.
ISBN 978-1-59523-040-9
1. Laffey, Steve. 2. Political candidates–United States–Biography. 3. Political candidates–
Rhode Island–Biography. 4. Primaries–Rhode Island–History–21st century. 5. Political
campaigns–Rhode Island–History–21st century. 6. Political campaigns–United States–
History–21st century. 7. United States. Congress. Senate–Elections, 2006. 8. Republican
Party (U.S. : 1854-)–Biography. 9. Republican Party (U.S. : 1854-)–History–21st
century. I. Title.
E901.1.L34A3 2007
324.9745'044–dc22   2007003971

Printed in the United States of America
Set in Garamond BE
Designed by Sabrina Bowers

In memory of Peter Bennett

And for the goodhearted people of Cranston who raised me.

Acknowledgments

My beautiful wife, Kelly, and my five children who, after a year of rigorous campaigning, endured four months of my writing this book. There is no way to adequately thank them—but thanks. I love you all so much.

Special thanks to Nachama Soloveichik (Solly) who worked painstakingly with me on this project. Without her talent none of this would have been possible. Her round-the-clock devotion (which found her at times curled up asleep on a combination of three uncomfortable chairs), her unhestitating devotion to the cause, and her penchant for arguing with me will never be forgotten. She is truly unique.

Paul Zisserson and John Dodenhoff—my two campaign managers who read and analyzed every chapter multiple times. You are both incredible, and I am greatly indebted.

Jordan Kogler, Jimmy Bennett, and Jackie Loscoe for adding their important insights from the campaign.

Norman Orodenker for his constant encouragement and accurate advice.

Jimmy Hackett and Joe Tatulli—for the space to write this and the colorful pictures that made the process of remembering that much easier. But even more so, I am indebted for their friendship and guidance.

Tom Marcelle—for answering my phone calls every morning from his office in upstate New York.

John Miller of *National Review*—for sending me in the right direction.

Special thanks to Bernadette Malone and the people at Viking Penguin who made this project a reality. Thank you for your support, your positive attitude, and for your faith in me and this story. Your phone call to me on November 3, 2006, was a shot in the arm to finish this project.

Finally, thanks to all the grassroots Republicans everywhere. Thank you for sticking to your principles, for never giving up, and for going to those local meetings that never seem to end. You are the only way back to the party of Reagan.

Contents

Primary Mistake

Who Is Steve Laffey?

I was forty-four years old when I ran for the U.S. Senate. The story of how I got there is the story of the American Dream. There is no other way to explain how a kid like me, the son of a toolmaker from Cranston, Rhode Island, who wasn't supposed to go to college, ended up running in the most-watched primary campaign of the 2006 midterm election cycle.

Unlike my opponent, Senator Lincoln Chafee, I had nothing handed to me simply because of my last name. The Chafees were one of the first five families in Rhode Island; mine was one of the last to get off the boat. My father wasn't a U.S. senator or a governor, but a blue-collar worker who sometimes worked two jobs to keep us fed and clothed. My great-uncle wasn't a constitutional scholar at Harvard University; my grandfather was gassed during World War I and later became an alcoholic. I didn't grow up in the best prep schools, but on Cranston's streets, while my mother watered down the shampoo to make it last longer.

When it came to tragedy in the Laffey household, it sometimes seemed like the old Morton salt slogan applied: When it rains it pours. I grew up in the Edgewood section of Cranston, sand-wiched between two brothers and two sisters in a traditional Irish Catholic household. My oldest brother, John, who was gay, spent his teenage years experimenting with drugs and alcohol, and would later die of AIDS. My other older brother, Michael, devel-oped schizophrenia when I was a teenager and has spent much of his life in a locked ward at the Institute of Mental Health. One of my younger sisters, Mary, followed suit. She has spent her adult life in a series of group homes.

Our house at 193 Shaw Avenue was a difficult place to grow up, with one brother trying to bang me over the head with a frying pan—and not in a friendly sibling-rivalry kind of way—and the other pushing me down the stairs. Before I went to sleep at night, I tied my door shut with a jump rope and piled my books at the foot of it as protective measures. To those who don't know me, it must seem like I wasn't very lucky at all. But in other ways, I was extraordinarily blessed.

HEROES

Given the instability of my home life, I looked for role models elsewhere. I found them, sometimes in the strangest of places: across the street, in the hockey-playing Bennett brothers, each one bigger than the next and almost all future NHL players; in the Ivy League–educated Norman Orodenker, who lived around the cor-ner; in my high school economics teacher; in Ronald Reagan and Milton Friedman.

I was thirteen when I heard Mr. Orodenker on the phone yelling at a public official: "I really don't care what you think . . . We're doing it this way!" Listening to him, I thought to myself, *I can do that. I can go to college, get a job, and yell at people.* Thirty years later, this lifelong Democrat served as one of my chief advisers during my tenure as the Republican mayor of Cranston and on my Senate campaign.

I was seventeen when my high school economics teacher, Paul Zisserson, showed us Milton Friedman's ten-part television series *Free to Choose*, and I thought: I can do this. I can be a Nobel Prize–winning economist. Twenty-two years later, Paul became my campaign manager for my first two campaigns, and Milton was the name I gave our overly friendly black Lab.

I was eighteen when Ronald Reagan was elected president of the United States, ushering in a wave of conservative thought and policy. I remember Ronald Reagan promising to bring the American hostages in Iran home and living up to that promise. I remember thinking, *Here is a guy who isn't afraid of being strong.* I remember Reagan joking—"My fellow Americans, I'm pleased to tell you today that I've signed legislation that will outlaw Russia forever. We begin bombing in five minutes"—and thinking, *Here is a guy who makes America laugh.* I remember thinking that if Ronald Reagan—a kid from Dixon, Illinois, with an alcoholic father—could make it, I could make it too.

Throughout my life, people told me I couldn't do things. I couldn't go to college. I couldn't get in to Harvard Business School directly from college. I couldn't become president of a southern-based investment banking firm because I was a Yankee. I couldn't run for mayor in Cranston. I couldn't fight the special interests in Cranston and win. And I couldn't run for the U.S. Senate.

When you grow up being told what your future holds for you, you can react in one of two ways. For some, people's expectations become a self-fulfilling prophecy. For others, they become a motivation for success, the fuel of a burning desire to prove the world wrong.

I guess you can say I fall into the second category.

After four years at Bowdoin College (scholarship, loans, jobs) and two years at Harvard Business School, I forged a successful career for myself in the world of investment banking, becoming the president and chief operating officer of Morgan Keegan, an investment banking firm in the deep South. At Morgan Keegan, I found new heroes: Allen Morgan, the founder and CEO, and his alter ego, vice chairman John Stokes.

Morgan is the mirror image of Reagan: principled, honest, and to the point. He had borrowed $500,000 from a bank and turned it into over $100 million in thirty years. His philosophy was simple: Take care of the customers first, and stick to your knitting. Stokes is a modern day version of Teddy Roosevelt and Peter the Great: all action and optimism. He was a problem solver in every sense of the word. If you had a toothache, he had a pair of pliers. Both Morgan and Stokes became major backers of my Senate campaign.

In 2001 we sold the firm to Regions Financial, and I came home to Cranston, in search of another mission. While my experience in Tennessee was phenomenal and I loved living in Memphis, I missed Rhode Island and decided to move home and raise my family.

HOMECOMING

Upon my return to Cranston, the third largest city in Rhode Island (or second largest if you include the prisoners, and I do)[1], the city went broke before my eyes. So I took the plunge and ran for mayor to help fix the city that raised me. I had never been involved in politics save a short stint as president of the student council at Cranston High School East and another at Bowdoin College, but I felt I owed the city a debt.

By the time I was elected, Cranston's bond rating had dropped to the lowest in all of America. Things got so bad that the state's only major newspaper ran a front-page story under the headline "Junk Bond City—East Chicago Lost a Steel Mill—Cranston, What's Your Excuse?" On the day I took office, the city was a month away from defaulting on $18 million of debt and missing payroll. This is not a book about how we fixed the city, but fix it we did.

When I was running for mayor, I had no idea just how strong the special interests in Cranston and Rhode Island were. The public sector unions and the previous mayors had run my city into the ground, much like they're probably destroying yours. The story of how we stood up to the special interests and fixed Cranston can best be summed up in one anecdote: the Cranston crossing guards.

Crossing guards, you say—they're just volunteers, some teachers, some kids, and so on. But no. Not in Rhode Island.

The day after I was elected, my phone started ringing off the hook. "Hey, Steve, my wife's been trying to be a crossing guard for ten years." Next call: "Hey, Mr. Laffey. The last mayor bypassed my wife for a crossing guard job. Can you help me out?"

It was the most baffling series of phone calls I had ever received. What was so great about being a crossing guard? It was like a bunch of obsessed fans trying to get Green Bay Packers season tickets. Turns out, being a crossing guard was even better.

Picture this—how about a job where you show up for half an hour in the morning, another half an hour in the afternoon, 180 days a year, and you get $129 per hour. That's $129 per hour, including $45 in cash, free health insurance for the entire family, sick days, holiday pay, and unemployment on the city dime all summer long. Sounds good, right? Where do I sign?

But these crossing guards, backed by the one of the largest labor unions in the country, the Laborers International Union of North America, were raking it in on the backs of Cranston's beleaguered taxpayers. So what did I do? I talked with my advisers. Many told me to let it go, that there was nothing that could be done because this was the way things worked in Cranston. Then I thought about the people I had met on the campaign trail, some of whom had no health insurance, some of whom paid for all their health insurance, and some of whom paid for half, but nobody who got it free for one hour's worth of work. And then I said: Enough is enough.

I fired the crossing guards.

All hell broke loose in Rhode Island. Over the next two years, a front-page legal battle ensued. In the end, we won, saving the city and its taxpayers $500,000 a year. Later, when I ran for the U.S. Senate, my opponent, Lincoln Chafee, belittled this accomplishment, but Senator Chafee, our "junior senator from Virginia," as one local radio host liked to refer to him,[2] wasn't in Rhode Island at the time and didn't lift a finger to help Cranston's taxpayers. While $500,000 out of a $200 million–plus budget wasn't the largest line item, firing the crossing guards was the first sign that business as usual in Rhode Island had run its course. As I toured the state to give talks, the Cranston crossing guards became a rallying cry for change in the state. "Ronald Reagan had the air traffic controllers," I'd often call out to groups of hungry Republicans, "and I have the Cranston crossing guards!"

After I was reelected in 2004, by one of the widest margins in Cranston's history, the city's bond rating made a historic recovery to investment grade. By January 2005, another mission had been completed. The city had a healthy surplus, the audits won national awards, and the budgets were realistic. Eventually, we would renegotiate contracts to bring historic changes, like health savings accounts for Cranston's policemen and city workers. By May 2006, Cranston was the only city in all of Rhode Island reducing property taxes.

ANOTHER MISSION

When I ran for mayor, I told the citizens of Cranston that I would stay until the city was fixed and healthy. So in January 2005, with the bond rating robust, I looked for another mission. I looked at Washington, and all I could see was the Cranston crossing guards on steroids.

The Reagan Republicans who came into office in 1994 on a wave of small-government adrenaline had become puppets of the special interests. Corruption exploded: the 2005 transportation bill was overloaded with 6,371 pork-barrel projects, the tax code was sixty thousand pages and counting, and the Republicans bore responsibility for No Child Left Behind—an educational behemoth.

When the free-market-based Club for Growth endorsed my candidacy in the Senate race, its president, former Pennsylvania congressman Pat Toomey, described this race as "the first skirmish in a very important war." He put this question to the American public in a *Wall Street Journal* op-ed: "Is Reagan's vision of limited government—the fundamental principle that brought Republicans to power—still part of the Republican identity, or has it been abandoned in favor of the seductive power of controlling unlimited government?"

The answer, unfortunately, was the latter. Nowhere was this malaise more evident than in the Washington Republicans' backing of liberal Lincoln Chafee. I may have lost the primary, but the Republican Party lost so much more. The party lost its reason for existence, and it lost its base. Without one, you cannot have the other.

Just a couple of weeks before the midterm elections, *Time* magazine summed up the sorry state of the GOP with this brutally honest line: "Every revolution begins with the power of an idea and ends when clinging to power is the only idea left." The Republican

Party came to power because it offered the country a brilliant vision for what it was capable of becoming. Ultimately, the party lost power because it betrayed its grassroots members and its own ideals. It was no longer "Elect us so we can cut spending," but "Elect us so we can win."

During the campaign, I received thousands of letters from supporters all across the country. One short letter from Betsy and Lyle Albaugh of Virginia moved me so much that I taped it to my wall. Read it, and then read it again. This is the Republican base. These are real Americans. These are the people we should be fighting for.

December 13, 2005

Mayor Laffey
Laffey US Senate
PO Box 8510
Cranston, RI 02920

Dear Mayor Laffey:

As free market Republicans, we're extremely disappointed with the current state of the Republican Party. Therefore, even though we're Virginia residents, you'll find enclosed a $25.00 contribution to your campaign to defeat the fiscally irresponsible Lincoln Chafee.

Starting with the 2000 election of President Bush and with each successive election, we've been increasingly hopeful that Republicans would make progress on the following issues:
1) **privatizing Social Security;** 2) **reducing entitlement spending;**
3) **reducing non-defense discretionary spending;** 4) **making permanent capital gains, dividend and estate tax cuts;**
5) **reducing tariffs, quotas and subsidies that limit trade;** and
6) **simplifying the tax code.**

Instead, they've made no visible progress on Social Security, vastly increased entitlement and discretionary spending, passed only temporary tax cuts, increased numerous industry subsidies and done nothing substantial to reform the tax code.

If elected to the Senate, we hope that you will work to achieve measurable success on the above issues.

Sincerely,

Betsy & Lyle Albaugh

Cc.
President Bush
1600 Pennsylvania Avenue
Washington, DC 20500

Senator Warner
225 Russell Senate Office Building
Washington, DC 20510

Senator Allen
204 Russell Senate Office Building
Washington, DC 20510

I don't know if President Bush and Senators Warner and Allen actually read this letter, but they should have. More than the voice of any overpaid consultant, these are the voices they should have listened to. These are the people who make up the Republican Party, and ultimately these are the people who will hold the party accountable.

This book is filled with many funny stories, but the message of this book isn't funny at all. There is nothing funny about millions of disappointed Republicans. There is nothing funny about hard-working taxpayers disgusted with their elected officials. There is nothing funny about Speaker of the House Nancy Pelosi.

Unless the national Republican Party changes its ways and figures out how to communicate with people like Betsy and Lyle (as I articulate in Chapter 10), the Republicans won't be controlling much of anything. And that's a shame, because I continue to believe, as I did when I was eighteen years old, that the party of Ronald Reagan is capable of accomplishing great things. It is a shame because the other party has become the party of Michael Moore and is capable of destroying great things. It is a shame because Reagan spoke about America as a "shining city on a hill," and right now, it looks awfully dark out there in the valley.

CHAPTER 1

See Steve Run, See Liddy Dole Run Scared

"After 10 years of controlling Congress, Washington Republicans have an identity crisis."–Pat Toomey, Club for Growth president, *Wall Street Journal*, December 12, 2005

VIOLATING THE ELEVENTH COMMANDMENT

The first thing I learned in politics was that there are a lot of people who will do anything to hold on to power. The second thing I learned was that most of them don't actually know what they're doing. This combination is lethal for the well-being of the American public.

When I decided to challenge Lincoln Chafee for the Republican nomination for the U.S. Senate in Rhode Island, I knew it would be a modern David versus Goliath story. A lot of people told me I was crazy. For one thing, running against the Chafee name in Rhode Island is the equivalent of running against the Kennedy name in Massachusetts or the Daley dynasty in Chicago.

John Chafee, Linc Chafee's father, was a revered figure in Rhode Island with a long and prestigious history of public service. Elected to Rhode Island's House of Representatives in 1956, John Chafee then moved on to become governor in 1963, secretary of the navy in 1969, and U.S. senator in 1976. He remained in the Senate until his death in 1999, when Linc was appointed by the governor to fill his father's shoes. For many voters over a certain age, a vote for Linc Chafee was a vote for the late John Chafee, even though the only thing these two politicians shared was a last name and a Y chromosome.

If the historical baggage wasn't enough of an obstacle, the Republican establishment made sure to put up a pretty big wall. After several futile attempts to deter me from running, it declared out-and-out war. When it came to defeating me, no price was too great and no principle too sacred.

The Cliffs Notes version of what happened in the Rhode Island primary isn't worthy of a book: we put up a good fight, and we lost, end of story. But there is a reason why our teachers didn't want us to read just the Cliffs Notes version in high school—the important stuff is in the details.

The story of my campaign is a story of how the Republican Party lost its way, and what it needs to do in order to find its way home. It is the reason why Republicans lost so badly across the country in the 2006 midterm elections. It is the reason why a ruddy Irish guy like myself with only three paid staffers who had never worked on a campaign before and a host of volunteers I knew from high school could scare the National Republican Senatorial Committee (NRSC) and the Republican National Committee (RNC) into doing the unthinkable: supporting a Ted Kennedy Republican like Linc Chafee.

What happened in the Senate primary race in Rhode Island was unprecedented. More than any other midterm race in the country, it demonstrated what is wrong with the national Republican Party today. It is true that the National Republican Senatorial Committee has a tradition of supporting incumbents against primary challengers. This was true in Pennsylvania in 2004, where George W. Bush and the NRSC supported Senator Arlen Specter over his more conservative challenger, Representative Pat Toomey, in the Republican primary. Indeed, I was informed of this sacred tradition when I met with Senator Elizabeth Dole at NRSC headquarters. The national party also has a track record of staying out of Republican primaries altogether, as was the case in 2002 when the Bush White House refused to pick sides in the Republican Senate primary campaign in New Hampshire pitting Representative John Sununu against the incumbent, Senator Bob Smith. But never before had the NRSC engaged in such virulent attacks against another member of its own party. Never before had the NRSC filed a Federal Election Commission complaint against a fellow Republican. Never before had the Republican Party used its Rovian tactics against one of its own. And never before had the Republican Party so blatantly sacrificed its principles in defense of a Republican senator so liberal that it was nearly impossible to distinguish him from his Democratic challenger.

But that is exactly what happened when I decided to run against Senator Lincoln Chafee for the Republican nomination in Rhode Island. The NRSC and RNC entered Rhode Island with their guns blazing, a violation of Ronald Reagan's eleventh commandment: "Thou shall not speak ill of another Republican." They were so afraid of losing control of the Senate that they not only offered their unadulterated support for a senator most Republicans despised, they poured millions of dollars into attacking my character and my integrity.

WHO IS LINC CHAFEE REALLY?

Who is Linc Chafee really? This is a valid and important question. Instead of using vital resources to bolster real Republicans ensnared in competitive races around the country, like Rick Santorum in Pennsylvania or George Allen in Virginia, the national Republican Party earmarked upward of $2 million toward Linc

Chafee's campaign. So who is Linc Chafee? What had he done for the Republican Party that made him worthy of that kind of institutional support? Astonishingly, the answer is: Zippo. Nada. Nothing.

It is no secret that there has been little love lost between Linc Chafee and the national Republican Party. We're talking about a guy who voted against just about every major Republican initiative. When asked why he was still a Republican, as he was often asked throughout the campaign, Senator Chafee remarked that he was a "traditional Republican," the kind who believes in fiscal responsibility, environmental stewardship, and aversion to foreign entanglements.

Unfortunately for taxpayers, Senator Chafee's version of fiscal responsibility entailed voting against every single one of the Bush tax cuts, even the middle-class tax cuts granting a family of four making $35,000 a year an $1,800 tax break. This doesn't sound like the Republican Party I know. Actually, it doesn't even sound like the Democratic Party, considering that Chafee was one of only three senators to vote against the middle-class tax relief bill.

Senator Chafee had a habit of being, in the words of the *New York Times*, a "party of one." He was the only Republican to vote against the war in Iraq, against confirming the nomination of Samuel Alito to the Supreme Court, and for amnesty for all illegal immigrants. He voted against school choice and parental notification laws, and was one of only four senators to oppose imposing sanctions on terrorist sponsor Syria. The list goes on and on. For more information on Linc Chafee's shocking Republican record, see Table 1.1.

But here's the clincher: Senator Chafee didn't even vote for President Bush. Before the 2004 presidential election, Senator Chafee wandered around the state of Rhode Island telling voters he didn't know who he would vote for and that his vote didn't count.[1] Although Chafee backed off the comment later, when

TABLE 1.1: LAFFEY, CHAFEE ON THE ISSUES

ISSUE	LAFFEY	CHAFEE
Taxes	Supports making the Bush tax cuts permanent.	Voted against every single Bush tax cut.
Estate tax	Would eliminate the estate tax.	Voted against elimating the estate tax; said "The wealthy are a good source of revenue."
Tax code	Supports simplifying the tax code so you can do your taxes in five minutes flat.	Voted to complicate the tax code by giving away billions of dollars in tax breaks for special interests.
Samuel Alito	Supported Alito's nomination to the Supreme Court.	Was the only Republican to vote against Alito's nomination to the Supreme Court.
Pork-barrel spending	Opposes pork-barrel spending.	Voted twice for the Bridge to Nowhere in Alaska.
Illegal immigration	Supports securing the borders first and enforcing the laws against employers. Opposes amnesty.	Was the only Republican to vote for amnesty for all 12 million illegal immigrants and the only Republican to vote against funding for securing the U.S.-Mexican border.
Flag burning	Supports constitutional amendment banning flag burning.	Voted against the flag-burning amendment twice. The second time, Chafee cast the deciding vote.
Terrorism	Wants to impose strict sanctions on terrorist countries like Syria, Iran, and North Korea.	Willing to reach out to Syria and Iran. Opposed sanctioning Syria.
Voted for Bush	Yes.	No.
Favors censuring the president	No.	Called censure a "positive" thing.
Abortion	Is pro-life.	Voted against partial-birth abortion ban; opposed parental notification laws and Laci's Law.
Gay marriage	Against.	For.
Church–state issues	Supports holiday displays on government property.	Referred to religious displays as a "charade."
School choice	For.	Against.
No Child Left Behind	Against.	For.

push came to shove, he finally wrote in the name of George H. W. Bush on the ballot, voting for a guy who wasn't even running, as an act of "symbolic protest."

This, folks, is the man the national Republican Party went out of its way to defend! This is the man deemed worthy of millions of dollars in national support—much of that money coming from grassroots Republicans like yourselves. This is what the national Republican Party has come to: a fatal case of power over principle.

THE ULTIMATE DILEMMA

Given Linc Chafee's abysmal record, members of the NRSC were faced with a formidable task: How do they support a guy they secretly despise? How do they support a guy they don't agree with on any major Republican policy initiative? The answer is: They don't. Instead, they attack the challenger. That is why none of the ads the NRSC ran focused on ideas or policies. That is why none of its ads talked about how wonderful Senator Chafee was or why Republicans in Rhode Island should vote for him. What could they say? Imagine an NRSC ad that went: "Vote for Linc Chafee because he loves pork!" or "Vote for Linc Chafee because he likes raising taxes!" Not exactly the message the Republican Party wanted to send. Instead, every single one of the NRSC's ads was a personal character assassination attack on me, filled to the brim with lies and distortions (more on that in Chapter 6).

In trying to hold on to power, the Republican establishment, both nationally and in Rhode Island, went after people, not ideas. Republican organizations attacked my temperament, my character, the stocks I purchased, even articles I wrote as a boisterous twenty-year-old in college. Not once did Senator Chafee or the NRSC offer a platform of ideas or a vision for what the Republican Party should look like down the road.

The Washington consultants will tell you that nasty negative ads work, and they will point to my campaign as a textbook case. Maybe negative ads do work, and maybe they don't, but this much I know: they do not define a party or a movement. They do not a political revolution make, and the Republican Party is sorely in need of a revolution. No political analyst worth his salt will tell you that Ronald Reagan brought the Republican Party to power because of the genius of his negative ads. Even Democratic pundits who secretly own Ronald Reagan voodoo dolls admit that Ronald Reagan's message was forward looking and full of optimism.

The NRSC and the RNC may have won the smallest of battles in Rhode Island, but they got there by conceding the larger war to their Democratic counterparts. The consequences of saving Linc Chafee in the Rhode Island Republican primary will reverberate across the country for years to come, as we saw in 2006's midterm elections. Already, grassroots Republicans across America are furious with the NRSC and are taking out their anger the old-fashioned way: through their votes and their pocketbooks.

When Chafee voted against Sam Alito's Supreme Court nomination, the number of angry comments inundating the NRSC's blog was so overwhelming that the NRSC actually removed the original post and all the angry comments from its Web site under the misguided philosophy of, if you erase it, it won't exist. Fortunately, a local Rhode Island conservative blog, Anchor Rising (www.anchorrising.com), preserved some of the comments for posterity before they were strategically deleted.

"Wise up NRSC. No $$ till you step down from your cynical support of this uber-RINO [Republican In Name Only]," wrote an anonymous Republican known to the blogosphere as Brad-maui. "I have observed Chafee's performance in the Senate and find no resemblance between him and a conservative," wrote another irate commenter. A Providence, Rhode Island, resident named Ballottra ranted, "You guys aren't doing yourselves any favors by ignoring this page. It's a dangerous thing to let angry people vent while you jam your thumbs in your ears and sing, 'LA LA LA LA!' Don't open an avenue of communication if you're going to blow off the feedback you get from it. I'm good and riled. And I'm in Providence." And Der Tommissar put it best when he wrote: "I have no idea why everyone is so upset. Lincoln Chafee is the greatest Republican since Jim Jeffords! Oh. Oops."[2]

Regular Republicans from Virginia to California called my headquarters to tell me how upset they were with what the NRSC was doing. Even after we lost, the calls didn't stop. One guy from North Carolina, with a southern accent so thick it made Liddy Dole's twang sound tame, called to tell me I had his vote when I run for president! The Republican base in Rhode Island and across the country rallied to the ideas and vision I put forth. Their support and outrage are an indication of what the Republican establishment sacrificed in Rhode Island. It shows how far removed the national Republican Party is from the very base it claims to represent.

The moral of the Rhode Island primary is this: The growth and victory of the Republican Party will depend, not on vilifying people, but on spreading the ideas of limited government, economic growth, a strong national security, and reform. These are the ideas on which Ronald Reagan won. These are the ideas that ushered in the Republican revolution in 1994. Without these ideas, the Republican Party is just a bunch of operatives slinging mud until they run out of money. And they will run out, because nobody wants to give money to an organization they cannot trust and cannot believe in. It is for this reason that, for the 2006 midterms, the NRSC raised only half as much money as its Democratic counterpart. It is for this reason that many wealthy Republican donors refused to renew their annual contributions to the NRSC. That is what the Republican Party has to look forward to if it continues to put its power-hungry ego ahead of its ideals.

A LESSON LEARNED

When I decided to run for the mayor of Cranston in 2001, I learned that the powers that be prefer handpicked candidates whom they can control over candidates who want real reform. Unfortunately for the powers that be, there is a great liberty in not giving a hoot.

It was December 2001, and I had recently returned to Rhode Island from Tennessee where I had been the president of Morgan Keegan, a major Southern investment banking firm. When I discovered that Cranston was on the verge of bankruptcy, I called my wife, Kelly, who was still down in Memphis with the kids waiting for our new Cranston home to be ready, and said, "Honey, Cranston's going broke. I've gotta run for mayor and fix this thing."

She was enthusiastic. The Cranston Republican Party was less so. The local chairman, Randy Jackvony, informed me that the party already had a candidate—Brock Bierman—a former one-term state representative who had lost the primary for mayor in 1998, but Jackvony invited me to come over to his house the next day to discuss the matter.

At the meeting the following day, the Cranston Republican Party told me that I couldn't run. Yes, they actually said, "Steve, you *can't* run. We already have a candidate."

I looked at them like I look at my three-year-old daughter, Audrey, when she throws all the shampoo bottles in the toilet (which she does on occasion). "When you say I can't run, is there something in the state charter that I'm missing? Is there a law that says I can't run? I mean, we're all American citizens here, right?"

For about half an hour, six of the eight members present took turns repeating the same mindless script over and over again: "You can't run ... We already have a candidate ... So-and-so won't support you ... The party won't give you any money ... You need the endorsement to win ... Blah, blah, blah."

Having been in the private sector my whole life, I had never learned the rules of Politics 101: Throw something—anything—out there, and hope it sticks. In business, it doesn't actually work that way. If you say something stupid, somebody usually calls you on it within the first five minutes. And if you keep saying stupid things, you're probably looking for a new job in a couple of days.

Not being a career politician myself, I didn't understand. So much for Politics 101. "What are you really saying?" I asked. "Are you saying ... you're not supporting me? That's okay. I'm running anyway. I'm just going to let you know right now, I'm putting a quarter of a million dollars of my own money into the race ... and I'll see you out on the campaign trail. No big deal."

After another half hour of this mind-numbing back-and-forth, the meeting took a shocking turn. Brock Bierman, heir to the Cranston throne, announced to the stunned crowd: "I can't have a primary ... My wife says I can't have a primary ... I just can't do it!"

As I looked to my right, tears were streaming down his face. I was concerned about what might happen next, but I didn't have to wait long to find out. To the amazement of the group, he stood up and said, "I'm not running. I'm out."

All but two yelled out in protest, "No, Brock, no!"

But he resisted their cries. "No, I can't run," he said, and with tears still streaming down his cheeks, he fled the house.

Now imagine this: I was sitting in a room with a group of people who had berated me for over an hour, telling me I couldn't run for mayor, but I was the only candidate left sitting. What does a guy like me do in a situation like this? I did the only thing I could think of. I stood up and said, "Everybody have a great holiday season. Merry Christmas, happy Hanukah, see you all later."

THE NRSC GETS POINTS FOR TRYING

To the credit of the national Republican Party, they were mildly more polite, at least initially, and nobody cried. They told me I *shouldn't* run for the U.S. Senate, instead of the more definitive *couldn't*.

The first hint of the opposition I would face came in late winter of 2005, months before I had made a final decision about running. I received a call from a childhood friend of mine, James S. "Jimmy" Bennett, a 2002 gubernatorial candidate in Rhode Island and a key fund-raiser for Chafee during his 2000 Senate campaign.

"Stevie," he said, "it's Jimmy. I just got a call from Senator Chafee. He wanted to know why you don't get along with him. 'What's wrong with our relationship?' he asked me."

"You're kidding me."

"No. Not kidding. So I said to Senator Chafee, 'Senator, have you ever spoken with Mayor Laffey? Have you ever, I don't know, picked up the phone and given him a call?' Chafee said no, he hadn't thought of that, so I gave him your number. Expect a call."

The following day, I received a call from Senator Chafee himself. The conversation that followed and our subsequent meeting is so astounding that you may be tempted to chalk it up to a little poetic license. But let me assure you, it is all true. I couldn't make Senator Chafee up if I tried.

SENATOR CHAFEE: *Hello . . . Mayor Laffey.*

ME: *Hello.*

SENATOR CHAFEE: *Um, I was thinking, uh, we could get together and chat.*

ME: *Sure, that would be nice.*

SENATOR CHAFEE: *I know you like to eat at a place, uh, Spoonums, uh, maybe, uh, we could eat there together tomorrow. Like uh, at two o'clock.*

ME: *Senator, they're not open at two, but why don't you come by City Hall instead.* [I realized then that the Chafee campaign had already started opposition research on me, and this was surely a sign of things to come. Spoonums is indeed one of my favorite local haunts, serving up the very best of two of my favorite foods: corn beef hash and johnnycakes.]

SENATOR CHAFEE: *Okay, I'll come by. Sure, uh, whatever you want, Mayor.*

I hung up the phone, shaking my head. Jeepers crow. No doubt, this call had something to do with the rumors of my impending challenge that were swirling in the local press, but what was this guy doing? From the little I knew of national politics, I expected Chafee to pursue one of two routes: either invite me down to Washington to wine-and-dine me until I'm so filled with food and guilt that I'd never dare bite the hand that fed me, or scare the living daylights out of me. I half expected Chafee to pick up the phone and say, "Hey, listen you SOB—you think you're going to run against me? I don't think so, buddy."

But Lincoln Chafee, the "independent, thoughtful maverick," took a different route. Indeed, calling it a "route" might be a little too generous. It was more like a meandering stroll.

It was a brutally cold day when Senator Chafee knocked on my office door wearing a seasonally inappropriate tan suit and duck boots. He sat down across from me, my oversized mayoral desk between us. His eyes flickered for a moment, no doubt taking in the display of books suspiciously (to him)/strategically (to me) positioned in his line of sight: my three-inch-thick Harvard Business

School alumni directory, containing the phone numbers of thousands of wealthy people across the country and a copy of *The Wealth of Nations* by Adam Smith. Also in sight was a framed copy of "Riley's Rule for Kicking the Complacent Ass," which reads:

> *Avoiding the solution of a tough, miserable, volatile problem is not discretion. It is cowardice. And it is robbery. Because as long as a serious problem goes unsolved, no team, no person can exploit its full potential. Any coach who doesn't kick the complacent ass on his team will end up kicking his own before long. (Pat Riley, L.A. Lakers Coach)*

I expected Chafee to get right to the point and spit out the question I knew must be plaguing his mind: "So are you running against me or not?" But I made the mistake of expecting Chafee to act like a sitting U.S. senator.

Instead, he sipped his tea, and we chatted about this and that, about how he liked being the mayor of Warwick back in the nineties, how I like being the mayor of Cranston, and so on. When he still didn't come to the point, I launched into my spiel about how much I love campaigning, how much I love raising money, and how I wished there was a campaign going on right now, so I could just get on the phone, start calling my buddies, and raise some cold, hard cash. I even pounded my fist on the table a couple of times for emphasis, all the while thinking, *Take the bait, senator—ask the darn question already!*

But Senator Chafee nodded politely and took another sip of his tea. At one point, to keep the conversation going, I asked Chafee what he liked about being a U.S. senator.

There was a pause, a hem, a haw, and then a classic Chafee facial contortion. After what seemed like an eternity, he answered, "Committee meetings."

I didn't know Senator Chafee all that well at that point. For a second, I considered the unlikely possibility that Linc Chafee was actually putting me on, because nobody—I mean nobody—likes committee meetings. "Committee meetings?" I echoed.

Another eternity passed, and he answered simply and, of course, thoughtfully. "Yes."

What was I supposed to do with this guy? I attempted to contact my executive assistant telepathically, hoping she would break in with a cat-up-a-tree or car-in-a-pothole emergency, when Chafee asked what was probably as close as the poor guy could get to a direct question. "Mayor, uh, where did we go wrong? Uh, I get this feeling that we're—uh, our relationship—uh, is not really in sync."

"I'm not sure what you mean, Senator," I answered sincerely, because I honestly had no idea what he was talking about. "I think you're a nice man, seems like you have a nice family. Personally we get along just fine . . . Do you mean policy differences? We have some serious policy differences. After all, you didn't vote for the president. You think cutting taxes is bad; I think it's good . . . I could go on all day. We have a lot of policy differences, but that's just business."

Senator Chafee didn't say anything, so I seized the opportunity to put this riveting meeting behind us. "Well," I added, "you're a nice guy, and I appreciate you coming in to speak with me."

And that was that. Chafee left, and I couldn't help but think, *This guy's a U.S. senator? They can't all be like this, or we're really in trouble.*

I was beginning to realize just how much trouble the Republican Party was truly in. Anticipating that Chafee was incapable of warding off a challenge by himself, the national Republican Party entered the fray on behalf of his political career.

In early spring of 2005, the full-court press began. It started with a call from Republican National Committee chairman Ken

Mehlman. He was polite, telling me to call him Ken, which I did. He also made sure to flatter me, which accomplished nothing considering that he called to convince me to run for lieutenant governor, a job that legally has no function in Rhode Island and basically involves riding around the state on a bicycle waiting for the governor to die. In fact, Rhode Island has a perennial candidate who runs for lieutenant governor every four years solely on the platform of eliminating the job. Go, Healey, go![3]

KEN: *I've heard you've done such wonderful things in Cranston . . . What are you up to . . . I heard you might be running for the Senate . . .* [Very subtle, Kenny.]

ME: *I haven't made any decisions yet, Ken, but I appreciate the call . . .*

KEN: *Well, we think it might be a good idea for you to run for lieutenant governor.*

ME: *Really? Why?*

KEN: *To help grow the Republican Party.*

ME: *What?* [Not "What? I didn't hear you," but "What? That sounds like a stupid idea."]

KEN: *We think it would help grow the party.*

ME: *Ken, you don't know me, but I'm just going to be blunt with you. The situation in Rhode Island is just this: At the head of the Rhode Island Republican ticket, we have a guy, Senator Chafee, who likes to tell the Rhode Island Republican base that there are a lot of Democrats in the state, and he's the best we can do. That's not a great message. So there really is no way to grow the Rhode Island Republican Party without removing the bearer of that message. What we need to do is change the leadership in Rhode Island. That's what will grow the party. If you have something meaningful for me to do that will really help Rhode Island and this country, let me know. I'm a man who takes on different missions, and I have no interest in just sitting around. I mean, Ken, you know Chafee didn't vote for the president, right? He talks about how the president has deceived the country, and of course, he didn't vote for any of these tax cuts.*

KEN: *I'm not calling you to defend Linc Chafee.*

ME: *Well, I haven't made any decisions yet, but if you have something that would really help Rhode Island or this country, I'd be happy to talk with you. But please don't go down this lieutenant governor road; it's just not going to happen. Thanks Ken. I appreciate your time.*

I got off the phone, imagining the conversation that must have transpired between Ken Mehlman and his bigwig buddies:

KEN: *So I spoke to Steve Laffey. He's not interested in the lieutenant governor position.*

BIGWIG: *Well, that's not good. Do we have anything else for him to do?*

KEN: *No, not really.*

BIGWIG: *So what's next?*

KEN: *I'll put the White House on the job . . . That ought to do it . . .*

And that's probably how I found myself talking to Karl Rove's foot-soldier-in-chief a couple of weeks later.

FOOT SOLDIER: *Hello, my name is Sara Taylor. I'm calling from the White House.*

ME: *Hello, Ms. Taylor.*

MS. TAYLOR: *Call me Sara.*

ME: *Okay. Hello, Sara.*

SARA: *We were wondering if you had decided what your plans are.*

ME: *Thank you for asking, but no, I haven't made any decisions yet.* [Why would I tell complete strangers my plans? Is that how it works in politics? It certainly doesn't work that way in business. I never walked down the street shouting, "I'm going to sell this stock tomorrow!"]

SARA: *Maybe you should run for lieutenant governor.*

ME: *I'm sorry, Sara. We don't know each other. What do you do in the White House?*

SARA: *I work for Karl Rove. I'm the White House political director.*

ME: *Listen, Ken Mehlman called me a while back about the same thing. I really don't mean to be rude. I'm sure you're a really talented young lady, but what about this lieutenant governor thing do you guys not get? You obviously must talk among yourselves. I don't mean to repeat what I just told Ken Mehlman, but, one, it's no way to grow the Republican Party, and, more importantly, the lieutenant governor has no job description and no official power. It's a nothing job. By the way, do you know that registered Republicans are down in every city in Rhode Island except for mine?*

SARA: *No, I didn't know that.*

ME: *Do you have any thoughts on something real and productive I could do?*

SARA: *Uh, um—*

ME: *Well, if you do, give me a call.*

I'm sure Sara Taylor hung up the phone with me and dialed the NRSC directly to report on her lack of progress, because a couple of weeks later, Elizabeth "Liddy" Dole, the senator from North Carolina and NRSC chairwoman, called my house late one night, waking up my seven-months-pregnant wife. When she couldn't reach me at home, she tracked me down at Cranston City Hall. Mark Stephens, executive director of the NRSC, called and offered to fly me down to Washington on the NRSC jet for a meeting with himself and Senator Dole.

I remember thinking, *Huh? The NRSC has a private jet?* Wouldn't Republicans be better served if the NRSC spent its money helping candidates around the country instead of buying its own jet? But that's just me. What do I know?

My executive assistant, Jackie Loscoe, took the call. She thanked Stephens for his generous offer and let him know that my motto as mayor has always been "responsible to all, obligated to none." "The mayor will come down to D.C.," she told him, "but he'll take Southwest Airlines to Baltimore and hop in a cab." And that's exactly what I did.

When I arrived in D.C., I discovered that, besides its own jet, the NRSC has its own outrageously gorgeous building. I sat in Elizabeth Dole's executive office along with Mark Stephens, who informed me that he had worked with Strom Thurmond back in the day. I remember thinking, Strom Thurmond ... Linc Chafee ... Strom Thurmond ... Linc Chafee ... politics makes strange bedfellows indeed!

Senator Dole was a paragon of southern grace and charm. "You've done such a tremendous job in Cranston ..."

"Your husband was a great public servant," I responded with all the charm I could muster, sans the southern accent. "I'm sorry he didn't become president ... I really admire what he did in World War II, fighting for our country ... I love his new book ... Please give him my best ..."

After about half an hour of yakking about nothing, Stephens turned to me and said, "We want to talk to you because there is some talk of you running for the United States Senate, and our job at the NRSC is to defend incumbents—it's the number one rule in the charter."

"I understand that," I countered, "but I'm a U.S. citizen, and I can make my own decisions about what I want to do. But tell me something—what do you like about Linc Chafee? Why would you defend him? You know he didn't vote for the president? Not only that, he thinks the president deceived the country, and he voted against all the tax cuts."

STEPHENS AND DOLE: *We're not here to defend Lincoln Chafee.*

That's funny, I thought, *because that's exactly what you told me you were going to do—defend Linc Chafee because he's the incumbent.* But I let that whopper of a confession go without so much as a whimper as the conversation made its inevitable way toward trying to convince me to run for lieutenant governor.

Excuse me for interrupting, but there is something I just don't get, and this seems like an appropriate point in the narrative to blow off a little steam. These guys are supposed to be smart, right? They're heading up the national Republican Party, so you'd think they would know what they were doing. So why did they keep bringing up this lieutenant governor nonsense? What about "I don't want to ride around on a bicycle waiting for the governor to die" did they not understand the first time around? Why didn't they actually try to come up with something useful for me to do?

I explained to them as simply as I could that the lieutenant governor in Rhode Island does nothing. I reviewed my background again—Harvard Business School, president of Morgan Keegan, mayor of Cranston, financial turnaround, the whole shebang, and put this question to them: "Do I look like a lieutenant governor to you?"

Silence. That's when Liddy Dole mentioned that she and Mark Stephens are both Christians.

I was stunned to say the least. To this day, I don't know what religion had to do with any of this. When the conversation faltered fifteen minutes later, I blurted out: "Hey, since we're sitting here, three Christians together, let me get your opinion. What should we be doing to help Linc Chafee? I've met with the man, Senator Dole. We had two thousand employees at Morgan Keegan; I know when people hate their jobs, and Lincoln Chafee hates his job."

THE DYNAMIC DUO: *We're not here to defend Lincoln Chafee.*

"But no, I don't think you get it," I continued. "He's not good at it. I mean, he's a nice man, but why don't you make him head of the EPA or some conservation thing—that's what he really likes—and then we can really get some things done."

THE BROKEN RECORD: *We're not here to defend Lincoln Chafee.*

"Okay, okay, I just thought that we three Christians sitting here together might want to help the poor guy out."

We schmoozed a little more before Stephens said they'd be in touch. I told them I appreciated their time, but if I decided to run, I would run a vigorous campaign on the great issues of our time.

Stephens was polite. "I understand, but we won't be with you."

Little did I know that "not being with me" would actually translate into "We will do everything and anything to defeat you, including lying, making personal character attacks, and shattering Ronald Reagan's eleventh commandment to a finely diced pulp."

About a month later, as things were heating up, I was given one last chance to surrender. I was sitting on a hill at a Little League field in Cranston watching my then-nine-year-old son, Sam, play baseball when Mark Stephens called, wanting to know if I had any more thoughts. Of course, I had lots of thoughts, most of which are inappropriate to say even a year after the fact, but I told him no. He informed me that they had conducted a poll and found that Linc Chafee had a better chance of winning the general election than I did.

"That's interesting," I answered slowly. "Just out of curiosity, was it a push poll? A couple of my friends got some calls that went like this: If you knew Steve Laffey secretly kills dogs and sells their body parts, would you be more or less likely to vote for him? If you knew Lincoln Chafee adopts starving children from Africa, would you be more or less likely to vote for him? Was that the kind of poll you did?"

To his credit, Stephens was honest. "Yes, it was a push poll."

"Well, here's an idea. I'm standing here in a Little League field with a bunch of what you national folks call 'soccer moms,' though today they're actually 'baseball moms.' Why don't I go do a little sample poll right now? You can listen in. I'll go ask everyone what they think about partial birth abortion—you know, Mark, when they pull the baby out feetfirst and crack the baby's skull open—and then I'll tell them that Lincoln Chafee thinks that's a good idea. I can do my own push poll right here and see what people think. Would you like me to do that?"

To his credit again, Stephens chuckled. "That won't be necessary, Mayor. But I'd be happy to show you the poll if you're interested."

"The whole poll?"

"No, just the numbers where Chafee does better."

"Let me get this straight. You're telling me, based off of a push poll that you refuse to show me, that I could win, but Chafee has a better chance of winning? Does that pretty much sum it up?"

"Yes, Mayor."

"Have a great day," I told him, and that was the last I heard of the NRSC until it reared its ugly head three months later in a series of vicious, hate-filled TV ads, the likes of which the Republican base had never seen before.

WHERE THE NRSC WENT WRONG

The fascinating thing about the whole experience of interacting with Liddy Dole and her posse was how pathetic the Republican establishment seemed. After all, they were supposed to be the ones in charge. They were the ones who wield all the power in the Republican Party. They had millions of dollars at their disposal and the president's ear. Who was I? I was just the mayor of a mid-sized city in the country's smallest state, with only four years of political office under my belt. I was the David to their Goliath, the 1980 U.S. Olympic hockey team to their Soviet Union machine.

Following my conversations with the aforementioned folks, I began to wonder: *Is this what happens at the national level? Does power trump ideology and principle?* Of all the conversations I had, not one involved a discussion about what I could offer them as a U.S. senator. They never talked about tax cuts, the war on terror, or spending cuts. There was never any acknowledgment of the bigger picture.

These conversations were designed to convince me not to run. If anything, they had the opposite effect. I have always been, even as a young boy, a guy in search of a mission. And Liddy Dole handed me my mission on a silver platter: return the Republican Party to the party of Teddy Roosevelt and Ronald Reagan. These conversations confirmed for me what I had thought at the beginning—that Washington was a mess, and our leaders, some of which I had great respect for, were simply not getting the job done.

The people I spoke with were not problem solvers, but players in a big game of political chess. They were more concerned with maintaining their grip on power than they were with the people who put them into their positions of power. In the end, the Republican Party lost both. I'm all for a big tent, folks. But there's got to be a reason why we're in this tent. And that reason was never given.

CHAPTER 2

"Laffey vs. Chafee: The First Skirmish in a Very Important War"

"That was the point where it dawned on me. This guy isn't here to be a spoiler, he means to be the next United States senator. And he doesn't intend to test the waters in the Republican primary, then see what happens. Laffey is going for all the marbles."–Jim Barron, *Pawtucket Times*, September 12, 2005

When I announced my candidacy on September 8, 2005, at the local Knights of Columbus in Cranston, Senator Chafee declared: "I worked with him to get him started in his political career, uh, but as I say now, now I'll work to end it."[1]

Almost a year later, Chafee would continue to beat this dead horse in our second debate. When he was asked by the moderator, WPRO radio host Dan Yorke, if he still wanted to end my political career, Senator Chafee didn't miss a beat.

DAN YORKE: *Let me go back to the thing that Mayor Laffey said about his September 8 announcement and your reaction that you wanted to end his political career. Do you still feel that way today? You want to end his political career?*

CHAFEE: *Absolutely. Absolutely. I, uh, helped start it, and now he's running against me, I don't know if it will end it, but it'll—I certainly want to put a bump in the road, uh, and defeat him in, on September 12.*

Folks, this line sums up one of the biggest problems we have in American politics. Unlike our founders—who were doctors, lawyers, soldiers, writers, farmers, and every other imaginable profession—politicians now view politics as a career. Nowhere do we see this more clearly than in Rhode Island, where then-governor Lincoln Almond appointed Linc Chafee to fill John Chafee's seat when the senator died in the fall of 1999.

When I heard Linc Chafee's line, I immediately thought, *Here lies the great difference between myself and Senator Chafee.* Unlike Chafee, who worked illegally in Canada shoeing horses before entering the family business,[2] I had a real career. For the past fourteen years, I had been working in the private sector as an investment banker and had a chance to live the American Dream. I left the private sector to run, first for mayor and then for the Senate, because I wanted to serve my state and country before going back to the private sector. Senator Chafee, though, seems to have thought politics was a career that he was entitled to.

Senator Chafee was also fond of saying, "Why is Mayor Laffey running against me? There are other offices he could run for. He could run for secretary of state. He could run for general treasurer." Not only did this sound incredibly childish, but it was also the height of arrogance. Unfortunately, it was accepted by the press as a perfectly normal thing to say, as if the Chafee family had the unassailable right to suggest what other American citizens should do with their lives.

Even after Chafee lost the general election to Democrat Sheldon Whitehouse, he took potshots at me, saying that I "chose for [my] own self-gratification to oppose a sitting Republican"! He rebuked me for refusing to take advice from party leaders, Liddy Dole, or himself. Whoa! If anything, it was Linc Chafee and Liddy Dole who had the gall to think that I or any other American considering a run for public office had to take advice from them. The truth is, I took advice from a lot of goodhearted people in and out of the state before I decided to run—most of them grassroots Republicans who wanted a real Republican to represent them. When was the last time Lincoln Chafee or Liddy Dole spoke to grass-roots Republicans and took their considerations into account? Chafee certainly didn't when he voted against Samuel Alito's nomination to the Supreme Court. Dole certainly didn't when she poured Republican-raised dollars into attacking me.

My approach has always been the opposite. When I ran for reelection as the mayor of Cranston, there was an Independent candidate running whose only claim to fame was that he wanted to keep a thirty-five-foot inflatable gorilla in his backyard. (Talk about a single-issue candidate!) He was endearingly referred to as Gorilla Man. I never thought to say, "Why is Gorilla Man running?" When the debates were scheduled, I showed up and debated him along with the Democratic candidate. I never said, "I won't debate Gorilla Man." Now, granted, Gorilla Man lasted only forty-five minutes into an hour long radio debate before having his mike shut down and heading off to the restaurant in the next room. But I never thought he couldn't run. This is America. Even Gorilla Man can run and get 4 percent of the vote.

But the bequeathing of power from father to son instills an entitlement mentality that was so prevalent in the Chafee campaign and runs rampant throughout American politics today. As *Bloomberg News* pointed out, four Senate candidates in the 2006 election cycle were "fortunate sons" testing the "limits of dads' famous names." These were Lincoln Chafee, Republican Thomas Kean Jr. in New Jersey, and Democrats Bob Casey Jr. in Pennsylvania and Harold Ford Jr. in Tennessee. In 2006, six senators were the children of former senators: Republicans Lincoln Chafee, Robert Bennett (UT), and Lisa Murkowski (AK), and Democrats Chris Dodd (CT), Evan Bayh (IN), and Mark Pryor (AR). Other dynasties across the country abound: the Bushes, the Clintons, the Daleys in Chicago, the Gores in Tennessee, and let us not forget Chafee's chief backer, Liddy Dole, who married a U.S. senator and then became one.

For Lincoln Chafee, running for the U.S. Senate was about carrying on the family name. Even his uninspiring campaign slogan, "Keep Chafee," was borrowed from John Chafee's 1964 gubernatorial campaign. Though Chafee bore an "R" next to his name, I can only surmise that he never cared about the Republican Party or the beliefs of the people he supposedly represented. Chafee spoke about unifying the Republican Party, but he essentially existed outside of it.[3] For one, he didn't actually believe in any of the party's policies. Two, he thought he could win reelection by courting liberal Independents and Democrats. He figured that Rhode Island Republicans and conservative Independents would hold their noses and vote for him because they had no other choice. He was the "best" they could do. The thought that a Republican would consider running against a Chafee was outrageous. For that someone to be me—a poor Irish kid who made his own money instead of inheriting it—was simply beyond the pale.

The closest I got to exploiting my last name was handing out Laffy Taffy candy on the campaign trail and intimating that the founder was a distant cousin who spelled the family name wrong when he got off the boat. The truth is, I told every person I met on the campaign trail that my dad was a toolmaker. Seriously, if you live in Rhode Island and you still don't know my dad was a toolmaker, you shouldn't be voting. I'm proud of my roots and proud of where I come from. For me, running for the U.S. Senate wasn't about a career or a birthright; it was about solving problems and getting things done. As I told a local reporter the day I announced my candidacy, "They want to be something—they want to be a U.S. senator. I want to do things."

THE NRSC FIRES BACK

Five days after I announced that I was running for the Senate, I began to detail, in my first television commercial, exactly what I wanted to do. Standing at a gas station on West Shore Road in Warwick, I laid out for the people in Rhode Island one of the central tenets of my campaign: "We've got record gas prices, and what are the Washington politicians doing? They give billions to big oil companies and keep us dependent on the Middle East . . . Washington is a mess, and neither the Republicans nor the Democrats are doing a thing about it."

The lack of a national energy policy to win the war on terror has been one of the great failures of the Republican Party (more on this in Chapter 10). It has been a failure of the Democratic Party, too, but at least the Democrats talk about alternative sources of energy. Granted, the Democrats, Chafee included, are mostly concerned with the fate of Toby the Grizzly Bear up in Alaska[4] and less concerned about the increasingly powerful Iran, but at least they're talking. The Republican Party, fearful of sounding even remotely like the enemy across the aisle, has been completely mum on the subject.

I like animals as much as the next person, and I am the proud owner of two dogs, a cat, and a horse. But I simply can't work up the energy to make Toby the Grizzly Bear a priority when Iran is building nuclear weapons and talking about pushing Israel into the Mediterranean Sea. What I do care about is winning the war on terror. I care about making sure that we do everything in our power to make it difficult for terrorists to hurt us, including cutting off their primary source of revenue. I care about making America safe, not so much for the bears and the caribou, but for our children.

———

My message to the people of Rhode Island was based on ideas. In the business world you don't get promoted by telling your boss why the other guy shouldn't get promoted. Promotions are granted on the merit of your ideas and your track record. But it was becoming increasingly clear that the NRSC didn't have any ideas to run on. The problem with Washington was not that Republicans didn't know how to fight, but that they stopped fighting for the things that mattered. In fact, when it came to fighting for all the wrong things, the Republicans in Washington were doing just fine.

Two weeks after I released my first ad—an ad that didn't mention Chafee—the NRSC fired back with and ad of its own, demonstrating, as the *Providence Journal* put it, "how concerned national Republican leaders are about the potential threat Laffey poses." Entitled "Slick," the NRSC ad asked:

> *Have you seen this guy Steve Laffey? In his TV ads, he complains about oil companies, but he's the same Steve Laffey who ran a company selling oil industry stocks on Wall Street, profiting from offshore drilling. The oil companies made a fortune. Steve Laffey made a fortune. Now Laffey says he will "stand up to the special interests." Slick. Steve Laffey. Laughing all the way to the bank.*

My first thought when I saw the Liddy Dole attack ad was, *This doesn't sound very "Christian" to me.* My second thought was, *Let's hold a press conference!* Standing in front of Senator Chafee's Providence office on Westminster Street, I ripped into the NRSC for attacking a fellow Republican when it hadn't aired any attacks against Democratic candidates anywhere in the country. "Now there's a real head-scratcher!" I declared. "You would think that with all the scandals going on in Washington, the mess on the Gulf Coast, and gas prices at an all-time high, they would have better things to do than come after the *Republican* mayor of Cranston!"

Republicans across the country felt the sting of the NRSC ad on a deeply personal level. It was bad enough Liddy Dole had gone after me, a fellow Republican more ideologically aligned with the party than the man they were supporting, but the NRSC went so far as to attack Republicans themselves and the values they hold dear. Instead of promoting quintessential Republican ideas, they actually attacked the very principles that make the Republican Party—and America—great. In the words of Billy Crystal's Miracle Max in *The Princess Bride*, "While you're at it, why don't you give me a nice paper cut and pour lemon juice on it!"

By attacking me for making money in the private sector, Liddy Dole and her cohorts were essentially attacking the capitalist system on which this country is based. They attacked the invisible hand of Adam Smith, the free enterprise system, and the guy who pulls himself up by his bootstraps to live the American Dream. Unlike the Democrats who condemn Dick Cheney and George Bush for making money in the oil industry, I think it's great. The purpose of my original commercial was not to go after the oil industry per se, but the spineless politicians who throw unnecessary tax breaks in the industry's direction. Digging for oil is a good thing, and making money off of it is perfectly fine. That, folks, is called capitalism.

A day after "Slick" hit the airwaves, the conservative Rhode Island blog Anchor Rising ranted about the "sheer stupidity of the ad's argument." "Consider these questions," an anonymous commenter wrote:

> Is the NRSC saying it doesn't accept the important market-making role of investment banking firms in the American economy? Do they want to return us to the days when investment deals had limited distribution and were typically only offered to wealthy people with the right personal connections? Why is the NRSC ridiculing the important role banks play in allocating investment capital that

creates jobs in all segments of the American economy and for Americans at all economic levels?

An editorial writer for the *Providence Journal* asked a similar question in an October 2005 article entitled, "The Danger of Throwing Gunk": "The National Republican Senatorial Committee," Edward Achorn wrote, "seems to have forgotten that it is Republicans who will be voting in the Chafee-Laffey primary. And when did they start believing that the profit motive is evil?" Thus, the war had begun, but it wasn't just a war against Steve Laffey; it was a war against the Republican base. The national Republican Party would soon learn that winning primaries isn't everything and that there is indeed a great danger in throwing gunk.

Shortly after the NRSC ran its ad, the Club for Growth released the results of a poll demonstrating that the NRSC ad angered Republican voters and made them more likely to support me. When asked whether the NRSC "should be spending money on this negative campaign, or should they be spending money against Democrats instead," an overwhelming 71 percent of respondents answered "Spend against Democrats."

From that day forward, the invisible hand of Adam Smith found itself tightly clutched around the NRSC's bank account as Republicans across the country refused to continue their contributions. For the first eight months of the 2005–2006 fund-raising cycle, the NRSC kept pace with its Democratic counterpart, the Democratic Senatorial Campaign Committee (DSCC), lagging behind by only $3 million. But from September onward–the same time I announced my candidacy and the NRSC bombarded Rhode Island's airwaves with attack ads–the NRSC's fund-raising took a sudden turn for the worse. Over the next fourteen months– from September 2005 to October 2006–the DSCC out-raised Liddy Dole and the NRSC by an astounding $22.9 million.

Obviously, my race was not the sole cause of NRSC's troubles, but it certainly played a role. I personally received phone calls from wealthy donors, vowing to contribute directly to candidates in the future instead of donating money to the NRSC. Following the GOP's massive losses in the 2006 midterms, Elizabeth Dole defended her tenure as NRSC chairwoman even though it proved to be a spectacular failure. "I can sleep well at night knowing we did everything possible to hold the Senate," she said. "All I know is I worked my head off, and that's all you can do." What a ridiculous thing to say. You can work your head off digging a ditch next to your house, but what good does that do anyone, especially if you don't need a ditch?

Worse, the NRSC actually went into debt over the disastrous 2006 election cycle. Liddy Dole sent the following letter, via e-mail, to Republicans in late November 2006, begging for donations to fill the hole she had dug herself into:

Dear Republican Friend,

I want to thank you from the bottom of my heart for your generous support of our efforts to elect Republicans to the United States Senate this year.

I just wish I could say I'm writing today to celebrate a Republican victory—but as you know, we were beaten by the Democrats in a very difficult election year for Republicans nationwide.

But even though we were unable to retain our Senate Majority, I believe we can still walk away from this election with our heads held high . . .

. . . Despite the odds against us, we fought hard in all our U.S. Senate races and still managed to keep the Senate extremely close!

And given how close so many races were, I even authorized the NRSC to go into debt so we could put more money into important Election Day messages.

As a result, the NRSC is now in debt after we spent every last cent on last-minute advertising and other efforts.

That's why I'm reaching out to the NRSC's most loyal and generous supporters like you today.

If you are in a position to do so, please make an immediate online contribution to the NRSC in the amount of $25, $50, $75, $100, $250, or more to help us wipe-out our remaining debt and make sure we have the funds to start 2007 with the maximum financial strength possible.

Click here to donate to the NRSC's debt reduction campaign!

I know you have already done so much this year. And I truly wish that I did not have to ask you for another contribution . . .

But if we let this debt linger, it will cripple our efforts to recruit great candidates for the next election and begin our drive to win the one additional seat we need to regain the Senate Majority.

So please, don't let me down—Help the NRSC recover from our election debt at once.

Remember, the sooner we can pay off the debt from the last election and begin to focus on the next campaign, the greater our chances are of regaining the majority in the next election.

So please help me make sure the next NRSC Chairman can hit the ground running in 2007 with no debt.

Simply follow this link: to help fund our debt retirement efforts with an immediate, secure online donation today!

No matter how much you can contribute, I want you to know that I deeply appreciate all that you have done for our Party, our Senate candidates, and me during the past year.

As my term as NRSC Chair comes to an end, I look back and cherish the great friendships I have made with loyal Republicans all across this country. I am truly thankful to have friends like you who are committed to our cause, our ideals and principles.

With my warmest best wishes,
Senator Elizabeth Dole
Chair, National Republican Senatorial Committee

Clearly, Liddy Dole's management of the NRSC was not that different from how the Republican-controlled Congress ran the country.

THE CLUB FOR GROWTH

The NRSC may have dissed the Republican base, but fortunately there were still groups out there that felt passionately about preserving Republican values and fighting for them. One such group was the Club for Growth, riding into Rhode Island on a white horse, complete with shining armor and money. Lots and lots of money.

Founded in 1999 by Stephen Moore as an anti-tax, pro-free-market organization, the Club for Growth made headlines when it backed Pennsylvania representative Pat Toomey in his 2004 primary challenge to the liberal Republican senator Arlen Specter. After his razor-thin loss to Specter, Toomey assumed the Club for Growth presidency, tripling its member size and supporting candidates around the country—Democratic or Republican—who shared the group's belief in low taxes, tax reform, spending cuts, school choice, and the expansion of free trade.

During the 2006 campaign, Chafee attempted to tag me as a pawn of the special interests, saying I received hundreds of thousands of dollars from "the Goliath . . . the great white shark of special interests, the Club for Growth . . . one of the most nefarious and infamous in Washington." I still laugh when I read this quote, especially considering the amount of money Chafee took from *real* special interests, including thousands of dollars from his beloved horse industry, the teacher unions, and pharmaceutical political action committees (PACs). The difference between these special interests and the Club for Growth is as wide as those between Chafee and myself. Narrow special interests, like the National Thoroughbred Racing Association, try to change tax laws to benefit a small number of people on the backs of the many. The National Thoroughbred Racing Association wins; the American people lose. In contrast, the Club for Growth represents the overwhelming general interest. They want to cut taxes and get rid of wasteful spending for *everyone*. That doesn't sound too nefarious to me.

I asked several questions countless times during the campaign. "Who doesn't want to cut taxes?" Except for Chafee, who's worth tens of millions of dollars. "Who doesn't want to get rid of wasteful spending?" Except for Chafee, who needed to bring home pork in order to keep his job. "Who is against school choice?" Except for Chafee and his limousine-liberal buddies like Ted Kennedy who send their children to the best private schools but deny poor children the same access.

If anything, the Club for Growth promotes policies that endanger the "nefarious" special interests Chafee needed to keep his political career afloat. Policies like school choice and tax reform strike fear in the hearts of the National Education Association and the National Thoroughbred Racing Association but are embraced by a vast majority of American citizens. In mainstream papers, it is rare to see the Club for Growth's name by itself, not preceded by the qualifier "conservative," but most Americans—Republicans and Democrats, conservatives and liberals—favor lower taxes, a simpler tax code, an end to pork projects like the Bridge to Nowhere, and school choice.

On Monday, December 12, 2005, I opened up the *Wall Street Journal* at five in the morning like I normally do before I work out at the local YMCA. When I got to the editorial pages, there it was. In an op-ed by Pat Toomey entitled "Laffey vs. Chafee: The First Skirmish in a Very Important War," the Club for Growth endorsed my candidacy.

Railing against the Republican establishment that embraced Chafee and "dutifully enforces an unprincipled, though ironclad, mutual-defense agreement that ignores ideology," Toomey saw what the party leaders refused to see. He saw a Republican Party suffering from an "identity crisis," a party that "gave us a farm bill that only a Soviet central planner could love; a campaign-finance reform bill that expands government's unconstitutional restrictions on speech; a prescription-drug entitlement program that Lyndon Johnson could only have dreamed of; and a transportation bill with more than 40 times as many pork projects it took to earn Reagan's veto." Comparing my primary race to the 1976 presidential primary between Ronald Reagan and Gerald Ford, Toomey labeled my race "the first skirmish in a very important battle," a battle for the heart and soul of the Republican Party.

In the months that followed, the Club for Growth ran many commercials and raised thousands of dollars for my campaign from individuals all across this great country. Though Senator Chafee ridiculed these individuals as members of a "nefarious" special interest, these folks were simply the people who make up the Republican base. These were people like Betsy and Lyle Albaugh, whom I wrote about in the introduction to this book. These were people like Harry and George, whom you will meet in the next chapter. These people were the foot soldiers in the battle that Toomey described. Without their help, we could not have gotten as far as we did. And though we lost the "first skirmish" in Rhode Island, the battle for the soul of the Republican Party rages on.

CHAPTER 3

The Team: Two Guys, a Girl, and a Whole Lot of Pizza

"If you build it, he will come."–Field of Dreams, 1989

THE REAL GRASSROOTS VOLUNTEERS

The National Republican Senatorial Committee tried desperately to portray me as an insider career politician. They sent out a mailer with a fat guy chomping on a cigar (I'm five feet ten, weigh 178 pounds, and don't smoke); a mailer implying that I was breaking open champagne bottles at city hall (I've never had a drink in my life); and a mailer depicting me scratching another politician's back (the only back I scratch is my wife's). Unfortunately for the NRSC, my entire campaign, from my policy platforms right down to my ragtag team of staff and volunteers, embodied the quintessential outsider campaign.

Case in point: The most important guy on my campaign came to America with one shoe.

Having been through two grassroots mayoral campaigns, I had a large arsenal of volunteers and supporters by the time I announced my candidacy for the U.S. Senate. But these were not your typical campaign volunteers. The vast majority of them were not political junkies. Before they met me, most had never worked on a campaign in their lives. They were just regular people—with husbands and wives and children—who wanted to make a difference. They wanted to make sure their children would grow up in a world that was safe, secure, and filled with opportunities.

In politics and baseball it comes down to the famous line from the movie *Field of Dreams*: "If you build it, he will come." In other words, if you have a real mission, people will want to be a part of it. Occasionally, we'd receive e-mails from the Chafee campaign (we signed up for the Chafee e-mail list and the Chafee campaign was never clever enough to take us off) saying: "Make 150 phone calls at the Newport, Warwick, or Woonsocket field offices on Wednesday, Thursday, or Friday, and get into the McCain event for free." In contrast, all of the people working on my campaign were there because they believed in what we were doing. They weren't looking to hobnob with important people or secure jobs for themselves or their friends. Most of them had jobs, and the few who didn't preferred it that way.

Many of these people were exactly what you think of when you think of grassroots Republicans. They were hard-working middle-class folks who were sick and tired of Washington politicians spending taxpayer money as if it were their own. They were fed up with the national Republican Party, which had control of the presidency, the Senate, and the House, and still couldn't live up to its own platform. Most of all, they were sick and tired of being forced to settle for the small ideological crumbs that Lincoln Chafee threw their way every couple of years. These people were just like you—regular folks who wanted to play some small part in making this country better.

THE GANG

When I first got ready to run for mayor of Cranston in 2002, I received a series of strange phone calls at my still-unofficial headquarters. Each week another phone call, each week the same deep Rhode Island accent: "Mr. Laffey, how dare you insult the gay and lesbian groups in Cranston? We'll be in touch soon." Click.

A couple of days later: "Mr. Laffey, I'm with the Italian Americans of Rhode Island. How dare you insult us? You may think you're a bigwig in Memphis, but we got news for you. We'll be in touch." Click.

The following week: "Mr. Laffey, this is Jim with the United Anglo-Saxons of Rhode Island—the UAS. We have a real problem with you Irish people. Who the hell do you think you are? Don't you bother trying to reach us. We'll find you, Mr. Laffey." Click.

After five calls like this, I began to grow mildly concerned. *How could I have insulted anyone yet?* I thought. I hadn't even officially announced for mayor, but there I was ticking off people left and right. What was going on?

Then the phone rang again, and a voice exclaimed, "Laff! How do ya like those crank phone calls?"

A lightbulb went off in my head: Eddie! It's Eddie! I hadn't spoken to Eddie in twenty years—since the days when we egged houses and played ding-dong ditch. Growing up, Eddie was a grade ahead of me and lived over on the next street. We were part of a group of twenty neighborhood kids doing things that kids do (but that you don't actually want your own kids to do). Out of the group, Eddie had long ago captured a special place in my heart. To this day, I introduce Eddie to reporters as "the only kid who brought me my homework when I had mono in the eighth grade."

I had given up our days of crank phone calls years ago (caller ID really put a damper on the whole industry), but obviously Eddie had kept it going. "I want in," he said. "I'm here to help." From then on, Eddie led the way. Throughout my three campaigns, he knocked on thousands of doors, always knowing just the right thing to say to people. And when it came to calling in to radio talk shows and promoting our cause, no one was better than

"Bill from North Providence," putting his early training in crank phone calls to good use after all.

By the time we got to the Senate campaign, we had Chuck Dacey, aka Ace the Dace, another childhood friend; Lindsay, my best student at the University of Rhode Island (where I taught the top finance course) and PowerPoint designer extraordinaire; and of course, I can't go much further without mentioning Harry the Greek.

Harry is a true American. He came to this country from Greece at the age of nine with one shoe, hence, the nickname that would haunt him throughout his youth: One Shoe Harry. As he got older, he simply went by Harry the Greek. He remembers people being hung by their toes in Greece, but you wouldn't know it. Harry proceeded to make a life for himself. He lived his American Dream. A union tractor-trailer driver for many years, he saved his money, bought a nice house for himself, and raised two children.

During my first mayoral campaign, Harry barged into the little shack on Park Avenue that served as my headquarters. After a quick meeting with me, this lifelong Republican turned to my campaign manager, Paul Zisserson, and announced, "The kid's okay. I'm gonna help the kid out."

From that moment on, Harry the Greek became an integral part of my campaign and my life, becoming my unofficial driver, serving as "Uncle Harry" to my children, making sure my lawn was mowed, and putting up Laffey signs all over the state. Over his lifetime, Harry had three heart attacks and officially died once, but he always claimed that God kept him alive to keep an eye on me. And I believed it.

In the state of Rhode Island, it is a well-known fact that Harry the Greek has no peers when it comes to putting up political signs. For those of you not from Rhode Island, you need to know that political signs in Rhode Island have become an art form. This is partly because of the state's small size, making it possible to traverse the state delivering them, and partly because of Rhode Island's brash, independent streak—everyone has an opinion, and everyone wants to share it. In Cranston alone, political signs adorn every other lawn, revealing people's opinions on everything from the U.S. Senate race to the Cranston school committee election to "Vote No on Referendum 1."

Political consultants tell you that signs don't matter, and for all I know, they may be right. But I wasn't taking any chances. So we peppered the state with massive Laffey signs everywhere Harry could put them. I also figured that if I drove down I-95 thinking, *Holy moly, how did Harry get that up there?* then no doubt the Chafee campaign was wondering, *Holy moly, how did Laffey get that up there?*

All over Rhode Island, evidence of Harry's handiwork (and my Senate campaign) were to be seen. On farms, on back roads, above major highways, on the sides of people's houses, in places where no one should or could put a sign—there was an eight-by-four, screaming-blue-and-yellow Elect Laffey sign. Spotting a new Laffey sign became a game for everyone associated with the campaign, adults included. And though I knew not to question Harry's magic, sometimes I couldn't help myself.

"Harry," I'd ask because I was dying to know, "how did you get that up there?"

He never betrayed his secrets. "Don't ask," he'd say, and follow up with a deep, raspy laugh that only Harry could get away with.

To Harry, all things were possible. And all things were ethnic. Like out of a *Seinfeld* episode, everyone was identified by his ethnic background, his marital status ("He's divorced, but he's okay"), or his relationship to the Greek Church. And like it or not, everyone had some kind of relationship. Even my Orthodox Jewish press secretary was related to Harry because, Harry said, "You and me, kid, we're both Orthodox."

As we went from town to town, gas station to coffee shop, Harry seemed to know every small-business owner in Rhode Island, and if he didn't, there was only one degree of separation. It was always "I delivered food here twenty years ago," or "I know your brother Jimmy—he's a good guy." Even when George Stephanopoulos of ABC's *This Week* came to Rhode Island to do a story on the race, Harry introduced himself, saying, "I remember your father from the Greek Church in Fall River. I met you, too, when you were a little kid, and you didn't get any taller!" Although Harry received no education after high school, his intuitive sense of who could help us and how was always on target. Harry the Greek put the Washington consultants to shame.

Like Harry, some of the other volunteers on my campaign were lifelong Republicans who wanted to elect a Republican they could be proud of. And a Republican who actually remembered their names. A dedicated Republican, George volunteered for Chafee's 2000 Senate campaign long before he walked into my mayoral headquarters looking for Laffey signs. His experience on the Chafee campaign had left a bitter taste in his mouth. It was a taste he still remembered when I announced my candidacy in September 2005.

During Chafee's 2000 Senate campaign, George did the kind of grassroots tasks that volunteers tend to do: he built large signs, spent countless nights stuffing envelopes, translated campaign materials into Spanish; appeared at every pre-debate rally; inflated balloons and decorated venues for fund-raisers; gave voters rides to the polls; spent hours holding signs in front of polling places (and never got a sandwich or a drink); contributed some of his hard-earned money to the effort; and loaned his tools to the campaign—a cordless drill, a heavy-duty stapler, a box of staples, and a post-hole digger. This was a big deal. "The spiffy preppy crowd may not get it," George wrote in an angry blog comment, "but when a man lends his tools, it means something."

The first time George met Senator Chafee, the senator shook his hand and asked his name. The second time they met, it was no different. And the third, and the fourth, and so on. Writing for a local blog, George explained:

[Chafee] lost me long before he voted against the Bush tax cuts. He lost me at a volunteer appreciation party after the election when I realized he had no idea who I was. He had shaken my hand at each debate rally and had to ask who I was each time . . . Chafee just never seemed to care about anyone outside his inner circle of people who are just like him. That would have been the end of political activism for me had I not met the future mayor of Cranston a little over a year later.

A year later, George walked into my mayoral campaign headquarters asking for huge Laffey signs to affix to the sides of his truck. He happily offered to park the truck in different locations around the city over weekends (and walk home) as a kind of roving billboard.

This struck me as a little odd, but I said, "What the heck? Sure."

And that's exactly what George did. In between my first mayoral campaign and my second, I rarely saw the guy. But when it came time for my reelection, like clockwork, George pulled up with the truck, signs reinstalled, eager to get going. This time, George's truck led the volunteers through the streets with enormous speakers on the back playing patriotic music and, in between, announcing my arrival as we knocked on doors and met with voters. Two years later, George returned for the Senate campaign, truck in tow, this time with the new F-350, bigger and better, and running on diesel.

TWO WISE OLD MEN . . .
AND TWO NOT SO OLD

Throughout my mayoral campaigns, I surrounded myself with personal mentors and close friends who served as my advisers. My Senate campaign was no different. The oldest and wisest of my advisers was a mentor of mine growing up. You met him in the introduction—Norman Orodenker whose personal loyalty superseded any ideological chasm he had to cross to stand by my side every day.

Mr. Orodenker was one of my original supporters when I decided to run for mayor of Cranston, but as a lifelong card-carrying Democrat, he wasn't too eager to tell his buddies. You know how the liberal establishment can be—tolerant of everything to the left of them, hostile toward everything a millimeter to the right. Like a secret agent, we referred to him as Mr. X, a nickname he bears to this very day, sometimes shortened to X, as in, "Hey, Steve, it's X here."

But as a secret agent, he wasn't that good at keeping his cover. At my announcement for mayor in 2002, he went from not coming so that he wouldn't be seen, to "I'll come but I'll stand outside," to showing up and sitting next to Republican gubernatorial candidate Jimmy Bennett in the front row—a picture that would be splashed across the *Providence Journal* the following morning. His cover was blown. But the name Mr. X stuck like glue.

The second in this pair of wise men was Paul Zisserson, my high school economics teacher and the person who bears all responsibility for introducing me to the market-based ideas of Milton Friedman. Paul was a lifelong Republican who had retired from teaching to head up my mayoral campaign back in 2002.

When it came to political strategizing, Paul was the go-to guy, but when it came to making coffee . . . I learned to stay far, far away. Paul had been drinking coffee as long as I had known him, so when we moved into our first campaign headquarters, I bought him a Mr. Coffee machine. A couple of days later, Paul informed me that the machine was malfunctioning. I wandered over, opened it up, and found it clogged with coffee grounds. "Hey," I yelled out. "Did you put in a filter?"

He yelled back: "Filter? Do those things need a filter?"

What did Cool Hand Luke say? "A man's got to know his own limitations."

The third fellow in this stellar group was my best friend and college roommate, Tom Marcelle, a Supreme Court–winning lawyer, living in Albany, New York. Tom is a brilliant guy with great political instincts, but unfortunately he has the technological mechanics of a five-year-old: a cell phone with no voice mail; a fax machine that never worked; and an e-mail address that went directly to the big black hole of Internet space.

We met our first year in college, two Reagan conservatives thrown together in Appleton Hall. Our futures would be forever intertwined from that day on. I remember sitting on the grass in front of our dorm at the beginning of our sophomore year when Tom told me that he thought someday he would have to get me elected to public office. So far, we're two for three.

Lastly, we had a guy who, for the purposes of this book, will go by "Fred." Fred is like the kid you knew growing up who could pull obscure sports facts and stats out of his head on a moment's notice. Where did Fly Williams go to college? How many Gold Gloves did Greg Maddox win? In Fred's case, his obscure facts were all political all the time. How many votes in the last

Republican primary? How many people live in Little Compton, Rhode Island? Who is the head of the Republican Party in Central Falls? Fred knew the answers to all these questions and many more. And when the press wrote, "There have been only two Republican senators from the state since the 1930s—Chafee and his father," it was Fred who jumped up and said, "Wrong! There was Jesse Metcalf (1924–1937) and Felix Hebert (1929–1935)—both Republicans." I had never heard of either of them.

These four guys—Norman Orodenker, Paul Zisserson, Tom Marcelle, and Fred—whom I endearingly referred to as my inner circle, played an active and daily role in my campaign. More important than anything else, they were always looking out for me. Their unselfish devotion and their constant availability (except when Marcelle was on his cell) made them invaluable assets.

On some mornings, Fred, perhaps the cheapest guy in the world next to me, walked to the nearest convenience store, read the paper, put it back neatly, and then called me to impart his daily analysis. When we had a question about how to respond to various press inquiries, it was always, "Call Marcelle. Call Mr. X." Every Monday morning I met with Mr. X and PZ to go over the events and plans for the coming week. Invariably, each meeting ended with the two ideologues sparring over abortion, but somehow we managed to be productive in between the jabs. All four would take turns playing Chafee in our debate prep. Of all of them, Fred imitated Chafee best, right down to his awkward hand gestures.

THE PAID FOLKS ... BUT NOT BY MUCH

It was great to have advisers, but somebody had to actually get the work done. And take out the trash. When it came to hiring people for my campaign, I approached this task the same way I did when

I worked for Morgan Keegan and helped oversee a company of two thousand employees. Even though I ended up hiring only three people, the philosophy was the same: hire people who believe in the mission. These were my requirements:

1. *Single. Sorry, EEOC.* I knew this campaign was going to be a twenty-four-by-seven deal, and I needed people who could afford to put in that kind of time. Besides, I have five kids—that's plenty for everyone to play with.

2. *Not too young and not too old.* Twenty-five to thirty-five sounded good. Sorry, AARP.

3. *On the same philosophical wavelength.* John Stokes at Morgan Keegan taught me this lesson a long time ago: Get rid of the people who fundamentally disagree with you. Otherwise they'll mess you up every time, and you'll spend valuable time arguing over things you shouldn't be arguing about. He was right.

4. *NEVER WORKED ON ANOTHER CAMPAIGN BEFORE!* This requirement may strike some people as odd, but to me, it was the most important one. I wasn't interested in folks who hopped around from campaign to campaign, but someone who believed in the Laffey mission.

Just when I was growing concerned about finding the right person to head up my campaign, I got a call from a buddy of mine, Evan Kirshenbaum. Back at the December 2001 Cranston Republican Party meeting, at which Brock Bierman dropped out of the Mayoral race (see Chapter 1), Evan was one of the few people in the room *not* yelling, "No, Brock, no!" It was the beginning of a beautiful friendship.

"I know you're looking for some help. I got just the guy," Evan said. As usual, he was right.

John Dodenhoff and I met in late June. He met all four of my official requirements, and one unofficial requirement: he had a great sense of humor. Luckily, he didn't need a job, so I put him to work as a volunteer. During the summer months before I announced in September, we sat together in an eight-by-eight room, rented for $50 a month, yelling into our cell phones, raising money, and gathering support. We raised a lot of money and didn't end up killing each other—two sure signs of compatibility. With that kind of success, I had no choice but to make John my campaign manager.

John was thirty-eight and the neatest guy I have ever met. Seriously, the guy gets a haircut every couple of weeks. Heaven forbid, one hair on that huge head of his should be out of place. We were the ultimate odd couple: I was Oscar Madison (a self-described slob) to his Felix Unger. We were the perfect team, complementing each other. I tossed half-eaten muffins over my shoulder, and John walked around picking the crumbs off the floor with his pinky finger.

In typical Rhode Island fashion—I know a guy who knows a guy—John brought Jordan Kogler onto the team, a buddy of his from the days when they both worked for the Boston Red Sox. Unfortunately, John left the Red Sox a couple of days too early and missed out on the $30,000 diamond champion ring that Jordo, as my kids referred to him, walked away with when the Red Sox won the World Series. At twenty-six and six feet four, Jordan was the largest member of our team. Jordo had a voice as loud as he was tall, and we'd often use him to drown out the Chafee mantra of "Six more years!" with our more original chant of "Six more weeks!"

Jordo became our finance director and campaign coordinator, which included all sorts of exciting duties, the most important being dealing with the daily barrage of wacky phone calls that came in from all over the country. As the campaign heated up, there was never a shortage of people who thought their little tidbits of advice and their angry complaints were the most important things we had to deal with on that particular day.

There was always somebody who wanted to know my position on an obscure topic. It might be a guy from Oklahoma who wouldn't send his $20 until he knew where I stood on banning assault weapons or a local fellow who wanted to know what I thought about the tax increase in Johnston. Then there were the experts and the critics. They knew exactly what we were doing wrong and exactly how to fix it—like the well-intentioned supporter who would have me solve the violence in the Middle East by creating a United Nations army. Or the fellow who recommended that "Mr. Lafferty" refuse health insurance as a U.S. senator until everyone in Rhode Island was insured. And finally, there were the folks with way too much time on their hands—like the Chafee supporter who called ranting and raving because some neighborhood kids had stuck a stake through her Chafee sign (smart kids). All these—and many more—became Jordan's specialty.

Jordo was also "Leon from Warwick," calling in to radio shows daily, defending the campaign and criticizing Chafee. Leon always sounded incredibly reasonable, pretending to be a regular guy even though he was sitting in our headquarters, reading off of one of our press releases. Leon even made a postelection appearance on WPRO's Dave Barber show, claiming, "You know, I'm a fairly moderate guy, but that Laffey guy, the son of whatever, he would never act like Chafee did."

We all had our quirks, and it should be pretty clear by now that I was no exception, but nothing topped Solly. By December, the campaign had taken off, and we needed a press secretary to deal with the onslaught of media inquiries. A couple of days after the Club for Growth endorsed my candidacy, John received a phone call at headquarters from a young woman wanting to join the team. At the time, it seemed like a bizarre coincidence or an act of divine providence. Just as we were wringing our hands over filling the position, this twenty-five-year-old novice sent her résumé to John, saying, "Nothing would make me happier than seeing Linc Chafee hang up his coat for good." Three weeks later, Solly moved into an apartment with no heat on Providence's posh East Side.

Solly's real name is Nachama Soloveichik. To this day, I cannot pronounce her name correctly. Apparently, the "ch" in Nachama is a guttural sound unique to certain Semitic languages and does not exist in English. After a week of trying valiantly to coach me, Solly gave up, and the entire campaign resorted to her basketball nickname.

Solly is an Orthodox Jew, which means she disappeared from Friday night sundown to Saturday night. I was okay with this arrangement, thinking it was good for Solly to get some rest over the weekend, but when she returned, she was just as sleepy! Solly has the unique ability to fall asleep pretty much anywhere—whether it was on three twenty-year-old chairs forming a makeshift bed at headquarters or crumpled up on the campaign RV as it thumped along Rhode Island's famously bad roads.

She always wore the same clothes—a denim skirt and a maroon University of Chicago sweatshirt—and alternated between the same four foods. Unfortunately for her, Rhode Island doesn't have any Orthodox kosher restaurants, so our headquarters refrigerator had to suffice. I remember walking in one day in the dead of winter, sniffing, and saying: "What the heck is that smell?" It was Solly, warming up her fish on the portable radiator.

Apparently, her last name—Soloveichik—is famous in Jewish

circles,[1] so every time I met a Jew I made sure to toss it out. "Oh, have you met my press secretary, mumble mumble Soloveichik?" All heads would turn. For the Jews, it was like having Babe Ruth's granddaughter around. Unfortunately, Rhode Island doesn't have a very large Jewish community. If only she had been Italian and the granddaughter of Joe DiMaggio, there would have been nothing the NRSC could have done.

With Solly's arrival the team was complete. Each one of the staffers was different in his or her weird way—emphasis on the word "weird"—but each one was thoroughly committed to the cause. Often you hear horror stories about infighting among staffers on political campaigns wrestling for power and credit. In that sense, a political campaign is not very different from a business, and the key to running a good campaign comes back to John Stokes's rule of hiring people who believe in what you're doing. John, Jordo, and Solly didn't join my campaign for their own personal glory, and they certainly didn't sign up for the pay. They came because, like me, their political awareness was shaped by Ronald Reagan's vision, and like me, they believed that the Republican Party wasn't living up to the terms of that vision. In contrast, our opponents hired three times as many people, and paid them twice as much. But I always thought that people on a mission work a lot harder than the Hessians who came in for the Revolutionary War. I was right.

Throughout the campaign, I met hundreds of grassroots volunteers. Many of these volunteers did the jobs no one else wanted to do. There was Ruth Ann, who came twice a week to make phone calls, bringing her teenage son Antonio with her, and my executive assistant and seventh-grade buddy Jackie, who always remained calm, regardless of the storm.

I could go on and on listing all of the volunteers and supporters, and believe me, they deserve to be listed, but that wouldn't be all that interesting to you. To all those who helped and contributed, know that your support was invaluable, and we couldn't have put up the fight that we did without you. Know that you are the heart and soul of the Republican Party, and without you, the Republican revolution of the Reagan years and of 1994 never would have happened. Without you, the Republican Party does not exist. Finally, to all those who would have liked to see their names printed in these pages, take comfort in the fact that you're probably just too normal.

CHAPTER 4

Selling the Republican Soul to the Highest Bidder

"Well if you really wanted me to go, I guess I would go. But when I got there, I might have to kneecap the guy."—Kelly Laffey, when asked whether she would campaign for a politician who didn't vote for her husband

Poor Laura Bush. I felt bad for her, I really did. It was a sunny Friday afternoon, May 19, 2006, at the Biltmore Hotel in Providence, Rhode Island. The crowd was filled with wealthy Republicans who had forked over $500 a pop to sit in the audience or $2,500 for a private photo session with the First Lady. Laura Bush looked beautiful in a tailored black suit, her hair perfectly in place. She smiled broadly and said, "I'm so happy to be in Rhode Island and have this chance to support your U.S. senator, Lincoln Chafee. He is an important member of the U.S. Senate."

And you know, you just know, the First Lady of the United States was thinking, *You ingrate—you didn't even vote for my husband!*

Laura Bush's visit to Rhode Island to campaign and fund-raise for Senator Chafee was one of the great ironies of this race. It was also one of the great betrayals. Throughout the race, Senator Chafee claimed that he had a "proven ability to get along with others," but his relationship with President Bush had been hostile from the very

beginning. Seven years ago, there were no smiles, no forced polite-
ness, and certainly no love lost between these sudden bedfellows.

In August 1999, when George W. Bush was still the governor of
Texas making a bid for the presidency, the press began questioning
whether Bush had ever used cocaine. On a Sunday morning talk
show, Chafee, who was then the mayor of Warwick, Rhode Island,
and running to take over his father's senate seat upon John
Chafee's retirement in 2000, admitted his own experimentation
with cocaine during college. The pressure on Governor Bush to
address the rumors continued to mount as Bush planned his first
visit to Rhode Island for a fund-raiser on September 8.

Two weeks before Bush's arrival in the Ocean State, Senator
Chafee appeared on the *Today* show with Matt Lauer. When
Bush's alleged drug use came up in the discussion, Linc Chafee did
nothing to downplay the controversy. If anything, Chafee helped
fuel the fire closing in on Bush, encouraging the media's witch
hunt and agreeing with Lauer that politicians who refused to answer these sorts of questions appeared evasive.

Governor Bush was not pleased with Chafee's national performance. In fact, Bush was so incensed that he refused to accept
Chafee's apologetic phone calls over the next week. By the time
Bush's plane set down in Warwick for the fund-raiser, he was long
past incensed and bordering on ballistic.

Waiting in the wings for his turn to speak at the fund-raiser,
Bush turned to his Rhode Island campaign chairman, who happens to be a close childhood friend of mine, and growled, "Is that
asshole Chafee going to be here?" When Bush was informed that
indeed the junior Chafee would be present, he pushed further.
"Well, do I have to fuckin' acknowledge him?"

"Yes, Governor," my friend replied. "I think that would be a
good idea."

"Well, I don't need him telling me how to handle the fuckin'
drug question. Who the hell does he think he is?"

Apparently, Linc Chafee thought he could get along without actually going along. Ever. On the surface, Chafee was all smiles and polite gestures, but when it came down to the issues that mattered most, Bush was better off counting on Democrat Ben Nelson of Nebraska than Republican Linc Chafee of Rhode Island.[1] Over the next five years, Senator Chafee proceeded to add insult to injury, voting against major Bush initiatives. Whether it was the war in Iraq or every single Bush tax cut, Senator Chafee was not so much getting along as he was ticking Republicans off. In 2003, he even went so far as to admit to the *New York Times Magazine* that "he has a hard time finding even one point of agreement" with the Bush administration.

But the biggest Chafee snub of all happened four years after the original version, this time making news in papers across the country. On September 20, 2004, at a science seminar sponsored by Rhode Island's major universities, Senator Chafee admitted to a group of top national reporters (1) that he didn't know who he would be voting for in the presidential election and (2) that his vote didn't count. Come election day, Chafee wrote in the name of George Bush's father—who, mind you, wasn't actually running—as an act of "symbolic protest" against the current Bush administration. If that wasn't bad enough, he publicly admitted to the *Providence Journal* that "his views were more in line with those of his colleague in the Senate," Democratic presidential candidate John F. Kerry.

If President Bush blew a gasket in 1999 over Linc Chafee's appearance on the *Today* show, I can only imagine the kind of profanity bouncing off the White House walls when he opened his newspaper the day after the election to find out that one Republican senator didn't actually pull the lever on his behalf.

And still, it got worse. If Senator Chafee thought it was high time to start repairing his relationship with the president, he had an awfully odd way of showing it. Instead, he went out of his way time and again to publicly lambaste the president. In December 2005, he accused President Bush of lying about the situation in Iraq. And though the White House had publicly endorsed Senator Chafee in the Rhode Island primary, Chafee had the gall to call Senator Russ Feingold's (D-WI) proposal to censure the president a "positive" thing in March 2006. In sum, Senator Chafee didn't have a nice thing to say about George W. Bush, except that he really liked W.'s father, George H. W. Bush. That's not exactly a ringing endorsement.

Given the litany of apostasies on Chafee's part, it's hard for me to imagine President Bush agreeing to the First Lady's "save Chafee" visit, let alone dreaming it up. In my mind, it was the great puppet master, Karl Rove, sitting deep in his cellar, the last bit of a cigar lingering between his lips, summoning the president for a top-secret emergency intervention meeting.

KARL ROVE: *Listen, I think we should send Laura up to Rhode Island to fund-raise for Senator Chafee. The guy's been out-fund-raised three quarters in a row by this Laffey guy. Obviously you can't go, Mr. President; people really hate you up there.*

BUSH: *C'mon Karl; the guy's a backstabber! He didn't even vote for me!*

ROVE: *Mr. President, we're not here to defend Linc Chafee. We need to keep control of the Senate. If we lose the Senate, the Democrats will start impeachment hearings January 21.*

BUSH: *Do we have to? Karl, this is really beyond the pale. He's a total traitor. He's been undercutting me since '99, when I went up to Rhode Island to fund-raise for the first campaign. What a backstabber.*

ROVE: *I know, Mr. President, nobody disagrees with you. But this is what we have to do. We're in deep trouble, and the guy's a horrible fund-raiser. He needs our help, and Laura is the person who can do it.*

BUSH: *All right . . . but he's still a backstabber.*

ROVE: *Yes, sir, he is.*

And with that, the president stuck another knife in the back of Republicans across the country.

We all know that in life, politics, and business there has to be room for compromise. Ideologues don't become presidents, and they don't become CEOs of major companies. We can all think of hundreds of things that we compromise on daily. In my family, it's usually over who changes my one-year-old daughter's diaper. Luckily, that compromise usually tilts in my favor. But there are moments in life when leaders need to take a stand and put their foot down. In the end, diapers need to be changed and decisions need to be made. Ronald Reagan's 1986 meeting with Soviet premier Mikhail Gorbachev in Reykjavik, Iceland, comes to mind. After responding "No way" to Gorbachev's call for restricting the U.S. space-based missile defense program, Reagan returned home, explaining to the American people that when it came to the security of this country, he would not compromise on our ability to defend ourselves. The press denounced him, but his popularity soared.

President Bush had a lot of these opportunities throughout his presidency but failed to embrace them. The day he signed the 2005 transportation bill instead of vetoing it, complete with more than $24 billion in pork-barrel projects, was one of these failures. Supporting Lincoln Chafee was another. Instead of begrudgingly agreeing to Rove's scheme, this is what Bush should have said:

Karl, I understand where you're coming from but this is plain wrong. We don't need to back this Laffey guy, but we should stay out of this race. There are a lot of vulnerable Republicans who deserve our help, and Lincoln Chafee isn't one of them. It was one thing to support Specter, but this is a horse of a different color. We shouldn't be wasting valuable resources and risk offending the base making nice with a guy who doesn't support the party in the most basic of ways.

It was bad enough that President Bush didn't stand up for himself. People expect a certain amount of self-righteous indignation from their political leaders. Every once in a while, when the situation calls for it, we want our leaders to be insulted and outraged. We want them to say: "You didn't even vote for me—enough is enough. You can't treat me like that!" But even worse was that President Bush didn't stand up for us. He didn't stand up for the millions of Republicans around the country who came out to vote for him in 2004 when Linc Chafee couldn't muster up the same support. In the end, it was these Republicans who took it on the chin.

THE STRAIGHT TALK EXPRESS TAKES A DETOUR

Over the course of this race, Republicans in Rhode Island grew accustomed to the troops of high-ranking Republicans marching through the state. Laura Bush was merely the first, leading an invasion of Republican celebrities to stand by Linc Chafee's side in the hope of burnishing his Republican credentials and filling his empty "piggy bank" (Chafee's words, not mine).

John McCain was one of the many marquee names; others included Majority Leader Bill Frist, Senators Mitch McConnell (KY) and Lindsey Graham (SC), and former Tennessee senator and actor Fred Thompson. McCain had so much fun in Rhode Island the first time around that he returned to refill the Chafee coffers in the general election.

But it wasn't enough for McCain to show up in Rhode Island and leave. Republicans across the state had to endure the sound of his voice for two weeks every time they turned on the television, featuring prominently in one of Chafee's primary ads. Even if you missed the fund-raiser, you could still hear McCain's lavish speech loud and clear from the comfort of your own living room couch:

> *Lincoln Chafee, a person who works at his job every single day of his life, a person who I know has never gone to the floor of the Senate and cast a vote unless it was well informed, well thought out, and placed the interests of the people of this country and Rhode Island first and foremost in his priorities. You can be proud of that kind of performance and public service. [Loud applause and cheering.]*

For many Republicans, McCain's Rhode Island appearance, both in the flesh and on television, was a defining moment. Even hard-core conservatives grumbling about McCain's accumulating breaks with the party over the past couple of years begrudgingly gave him props for sticking to his guns on Iraq and pork-barrel spending. But standing in Chafee's backyard, telling Republicans to "do everything you can to keep this outstanding leader as a member of the United States Senate," while Chafee conversely boasted of his vote against Iraq and his ability to bring the bacon home, was too hypocritical to bear.

If McCain had any chance of winning the Republican base in the 2008 presidential election, he lost it in Rhode Island. Perhaps supporting Lincoln Chafee was his way of kissing up to the establishment figures in the hope that the NRSC and RNC would return the favor two years later. This was poor political analysis on his part, because the establishment types have short memories, as evidenced by their support for Chafee. For them, it's all about "What can you do for me today?" On the other hand, the Republican base has a long memory, and few will forget the picture of a smiling McCain standing next to a khaki-clad Senator Chafee, proclaiming his support for the Senate's most liberal Republican from one side of his mouth and declaring himself a conservative from the other.[2]

And just in case some folks actually need a reminder, there will be plenty of those as the 2008 season heats up. Several wealthy conservatives called my headquarters during the race requesting tapes of the Chafee-McCain fund-raiser as it appeared on local TV, planning to use the footage in South Carolina in 2008. I can only imagine what these commercials will look like:

John McCain says he represents the true values of the Republican Party when he is in South Carolina, but when he's up in the liberal bastion of Rhode Island [cut to clip of McCain next to Chafee], he supported Linc Chafee, a senator who voted for partial-birth abortion, for amnesty for illegal aliens, and for higher taxes for everyone. John McCain—he'll say anything to anybody. Looks like the Straight Talk Express just ran out of gas. [Clip of the Straight Talk Express sputtering, coming to a halt, and collapsing as its wheels fall off.]

McCain's "straight talk" propelled him to celebrity status in political circles, but many Republicans don't hear straight talk; they just hear noise. If the shortest distance between two points is a straight line, then the shortest distance between the U.S. Senate and the White House appears to be one big zigzag. As Stephen Colbert of the *Colbert Report* pointed out in a politically themed reenactment of *The Lord of the Rings*, McCain is Gollum because "you don't know who he's really working for."

DESPERATE TIMES CALL FOR DESPERATE MEASURES

Unlike the aforementioned political celebrities, Liddy Dole never made an appearance in Rhode Island on Senator Chafee's behalf. Maybe three people at a Liddy Dole–chaired fund-raiser wouldn't have been the best story. Maybe the NRSC jet was too big to land in tiny ol' Rhode Island. Either way, the NRSC chairwoman made her determination to defeat me all too clear even without showing up in the flesh. The long arm of Liddy Dole stretched all the way to Rhode Island.

My race was quickly becoming a catalog of things that have never happened before in political history. The ads against me were a first. But the biggest surprise of all was a Federal Election Commission (FEC) complaint filed against me by the NRSC in early July 2006. When news of the complaint broke, reporters from all over the country started calling, not because the content of the complaint was all that interesting, but because, they told me, "nothing like this has ever happened before." When questioned by the insider Washington paper *The Hill*, FEC lawyers "could not recall a party leveling a complaint against a candidate of the same affiliation." It was becoming abundantly clear that neither principle nor precedent was enough to restrain Liddy Dole and her cronies.

At issue was a letter I sent out as the mayor of Cranston to all of the city's taxpaying citizens. The letter was sent along with the annual tax bill and touted many of the accomplishments my administration had achieved over the past year, including the fact that Cranston was the only city in Rhode Island to cut property taxes.

Historically, this letter was nothing new. Every year for well over fifty years, the mayor of Cranston has sent a letter to its taxpaying citizens detailing the past year's accomplishments. The only difference between my letter and previous letters was that my letter actually cost less. Instead of sending the annual letter as a separate mailing, I included the letter with the annual tax bill in order to save taxpayers tens of thousands of dollars in unnecessary postage fees.

Liddy Dole got hold of the letter and before you could say boo, the NRSC had filed a complaint with the FEC, claiming that my mayoral mailing constituted a "patently political communication" and should therefore be paid for by my Senate campaign, even though it made no reference to my U.S. Senate race, was no different from the mailings I had sent out in previous years, and was certainly no different from the letters Cranston's mayors had sent out over the past half a century.

But don't just take my word for it. Below, I have included a copy of the letter as it was sent to taxpayers across Cranston. Was this letter self-congratulatory? A little. Was it bold? Sure. Was it informative? Absolutely. But did it have anything to do with my U.S. Senate race? You tell me. Read the letter—read it five times if necessary—and tell me whether you find any mention of my Senate race or my opponent.

May 25, 2006

Dear Fellow Taxpayer:

GOOD NEWS!!! WE ARE REDUCING TAXES BY 1.5%. LET ME REPEAT—TAXES ARE REDUCED 1.5%!!! As you know, last year we were able to freeze taxes, and this year we have lowered them while continuing to finance the pension and health care retirement fund, increase the Rainy Day Fund, and still budget a prudent tax collection rate! **A quick glance at the back of this letter will provide you with a comparison to other cities and towns throughout Rhode Island.**

You will see that while other towns are raising taxes, some by astronomical percentages, the City of Cranston is the only municipality cutting taxes. Together, we have much to be proud of!

I am humbled and honored to have served as your Mayor over the past four years. When I signed up for the job, I did so with the sole intent of putting Cranston back on its feet, and I am happy to say that together, we have succeeded beyond our expectations! Consider what our city looked like four years ago, and what it looks like today:

HIGHLIGHTS

PRE-LAFFEY ADMINISTRATION	TODAY
Deficit of $11.7 million—about to miss payroll, default on debt	**Surplus** of nearly $20 million— largest in RI, including the State
Pension assets: $9 million and scheduled to go to zero	**Pension assets:** Nearly $40 million! Continually funded
Bond Rating: LOWEST IN AMERICA	**Bond Rating:** Up five notches **Investment Grade** Fastest turnaround in the Nation
Municipal Contracts: Free health care	**Municipal Contracts:** Teamsters/City workers—20% co-pay by term of contract
Crossing Guards: $129.00 per hour cost to the taxpayers	**New Crossing Guard Program:** $16.00 per hour with increased services. (A savings of **$500,000 per year**—or $5.7 million present day value!)

Folks, I love this city. When I saw Cranston on the verge of bankruptcy, I felt obligated to save the City that raised me. I thank all of you for entrusting me with such a critical job and for staying the course as we staved off the special-interests who tried to destroy our home.

I will not be your Mayor next year. As such, I have one final request from all of you. BE VIGILANT. Remember that the same special interests who nearly destroyed our city before will never go away. Below, I am enclosing a cut out for you to paste on your refrigerators. It is a list of warning signs so you can know when trouble is on the way. If you see any of the items on the list occurring, you will know to stand up and fight back.

Again, I thank all of you for giving me the opportunity to be your Mayor and to save this city that we all love so much.

As always, fighting for you,

Stephen P. Laffey
Mayor

MAYOR LAFFEY'S WARNING SIGNS

Not Funding Pensions . . . . ☠

Late Audits (Due Dec. 31st) . . . . ☠

Raiding the Rainy Day Fund . . . . ☠

Bad Contracts/Free Health Care . . . . . ☠

Unrealistic Tax Collection Forecasts . . ☠

When pressed by reporters and local radio hosts to explain where exactly the FEC violation had occurred, the NRSC spokesperson claimed that my use of the skull-and-crossbones icon and my standard signature line, "fighting for you," were examples of "patently political communication."

When I try to look at the skulls and crossbones in a detached, objective manner, three things come to mind: old-time pirates, the Oakland Raiders football team, and "Don't drink the stuff below your bathroom sink or you might die." Obviously, none of the above three items had anything to do with my U.S. Senate race or Senator Lincoln Chafee.

As for my signature line, "fighting for you," it is true that I sometimes used that line on the campaign trail, but this line preceded my Senate race, born in the early days of my first mayoral campaign and found on every single one of my past letters. As I told a local radio host in Rhode Island, "It's not a campaign slogan at all; it's sort of like Ronald Reagan saying at the end of every speech, 'God Bless America.' "

Instead of "patently political communication," what we had here was a bad case of patently political desperation. No doubt, the NRSC was doing its own internal polls on the Rhode Island primary, and they weren't turning cartwheels over the results. There's no other reason to explain why Liddy Dole aligned herself with the Democrats on Cranston's city council in filing this complaint.[3]

ANOTHER TIME FOR CHOOSING

I got into this race because I believed in certain principles and because I believed those principles were worth fighting for. As I watched George W. Bush, Liddy Dole, John McCain, and company bending over backwards to make nice with a senator who stabbed them in the back so many times it was hard to see where one wound ended and another began, I wondered, *At what point are the sacrifices we make in defense of those principles no longer worthwhile? At what point are we cutting off our nose to spite our face, and at what point are we saving our face from our nose?* The answer was clear. It was clear to me, and it was clear to the thousands of Republicans across the country revolting against their own leaders: when you sacrifice the very principles you claim to be defending.

In the end, it came down to Pat Toomey's question: what kind of party did the Republican Party want to be? It was a soul-searching moment for President Bush and the national Republicans. It was an opportunity for them to look in the mirror and say, "Who are we? What do we stand for? Do we stand for power or do we stand for the principles that brought this party to power in the first place?"

In his nominating speech for Barry Goldwater in 1964, Reagan declared the moment "a time for choosing." "This is the issue of this election," Reagan said. "Whether we believe in our capacity for self-government or whether we abandon the American revolution and confess that a little intellectual elite in a far-distant capitol can plan our lives for us better than we can plan them ourselves." For our national leaders, this election was another time for choosing. Unfortunately, they made the wrong choice.

Over the past six years, the Republican base has put up with a lot, and it will only grant its leaders so many get-out-of-jail-free cards. Many Republicans grew disgusted long before Liddy Dole ran her first ad attacking me for promoting oil stocks.

In 2005, blogger Ed Morrissey of Captain's Quarters (www. captainsquartersblog.com) started a grassroots campaign against the NRSC entitled "Not One Dime," in which he encouraged disgusted supporters to return NRSC solicitations with nine pennies to illustrate that they would no longer donate even a dime to an organization that couldn't get its judicial nominees past a trigger-happy filibustering minority. In a May 29, 2005, post, Morrissey wrote: "People like me worked our hearts out to give the Republicans a solid majority in the Senate so that they could lead, especially on judicial nominations. Instead, we have leadership that has proven itself unable or unwilling to rise to the task they themselves set in the election." Or as another irate blogger wrote: "If the Republican Leadership can't find their spine, I can't find my wallet."

Maybe if the party's leaders hadn't failed on spending, maybe if they hadn't surrendered on immigration, maybe if they hadn't been weak on education, corruption, and judges—maybe then supporting Chafee could have been forgiven. Maybe then Laura Bush's praise of Senator Chafee as a "passionate advocate" for taxpayers could have been stomached with an angry grunt and a drunken night on the town. But the establishment's backing of Chafee was merely the latest offense in a long catalog of ideological sins. Support for Chafee was not a moment of weakness or an aberration due to extenuating circumstances, but a symptom of a greater malaise, rotting the Republican Party at its core. It was a sign that our leaders had not only turned their backs on Republican values, they had turned their backs on Republicans. It was a sign that they had stopped listening; the sound of their own egos was simply too loud. For true believers, the Republican Party's support for Chafee was merely the straw that broke the elephant's back.

CHAPTER 5

The Important Issues:
Pixelation, Monkeys, and Leather Seats

"If Thomas Edison invented electric light today, Dan Rather would report it on CBS News as 'candle making industry threatened.'"–Newt Gingrich

When it comes to the most important issues facing our country, things like national security, energy independence, and taxes usually top people's lists. When I decided to run, that's what I thought, too. That's why I sat down and put together in-depth PowerPoint policy presentations on four major issues: energy independence, spending, prescription drugs, and taxes. These policy briefs were twenty-eight to forty-four pages long and involved months of research and planning. I also compiled two binders full of research on a host of important issues from Social Security to education to immigration.

My opponent and the NRSC thought otherwise. And so did the local press. After all, who cares about rising gas prices or the threat of a nuclear Iran when my mayor's car came with a leather interior?[1] Who cares about the $24 billion in pork-barrel spending and the $223 million for the Bridge to Nowhere that Lincoln Chafee voted for *twice* when the United States of America is grappling with the pressing issue of whether or not God actually told me to run for mayor of Cranston, Rhode Island? And who cares about cutting taxes and stimulating economic growth when a

Rhode Island columnist is wrestling with this stunner of a question: Why does my son, Samuel, age ten, like to wear military outfits?

I kid you not. A Rhode Island columnist actually asked me that on primary day. As reporters from around the country were sticking microphones in my face, quizzing me with questions about turnout and the NRSC's dirty attack ads, this local journalist desperately needed to know why my ten-year-old son likes to wear military fatigues. The answer, of course, was: *He's ten years old.*

But I get ahead of myself.

Senator Chafee and the National Republican Senatorial Committee realized early on that they could not run a campaign on ideas. They could not defend Chafee's liberal record, and they could not offer Rhode Island voters a compelling reason to vote for Senator Chafee. Their entire campaign was focused on demonizing me and turning the U.S. Senate race into a huge slime fest.

Unfortunately for my opponents, there weren't too many skeletons lurking in the closet. That left the NRSC and company with one of two choices: either dig up whatever you can or lie. In the end, the NRSC and the Chafee campaign satisfied their bloodthirstiness with both options. If you've followed races around the country, you've seen examples of these tactics—George Allen's dip into Jim Webb's fiction novels comes to mind—but of course these tactics were targeted at members of the opposite party, not members of the same party.

Three weeks before primary day and a day before the final debate, reporters at the *Providence Journal* received an anonymous package containing twenty-year-old copies of the *Bowdoin Patriot*, including columns I wrote as an undergraduate at Bowdoin College. These contained the boisterous rants of a twenty-year-old Reagan-loving conservative, riled up by the leftist domination on campus.

The goal was not just to persuade but also to infuriate the other side. Unlike Chafee, who admitted to using cocaine in college, I never drank or did drugs. Instead, I engaged in political outrage, a petty crime by my standards. But to the Chafee campaign and the NRSC, this twenty-year-old column–under the banner of "humor"–was supposed to prove that I was not suited for the U.S. Senate:

> *Why is the pop music of today so bad? Because it is Communist to the very core. It's turning the children of America into sissies and preying on the minds of every American, making them weaker and weaker. And how about this humanoid (I'd hesitate to say person, and I would never use the word MAN) Boy George. It wears girl's clothes and puts on makeup. When I hear it sing, "Do you really want to hurt me, do you really want to make me cry," I say to myself, YES, I want to punch your lights out, pal, and break your ribs. I say let's get those pinkos out of the music business and replace them with some tough conservatives.*

To be sure, these columns were provocative, as they were meant to be, and admittedly insensitive. The political climate at Bowdoin was similar to many universities around the country during the 1980s. The liberals attacked, and the Reagan conservatives fired back with everything they had in their arsenal. Ultimately, the back-and-forth sorties morphed into a competition of outrageousness between the conservative *Bowdoin Patriot* and the liberal standard-bearer, the *Bowdoin Orient.*

But that is beside the point. These columns were completely irrelevant to the Senate race and sending them to the *Providence Journal* was clearly a sign of a desperate campaign. It doesn't take a Harvard MBA to figure out who anonymously dropped the columns off for *Providence Journal* reporters to feast on or why they did. During our last debate, Chafee disavowed responsibility "to his knowledge," so that left only one option. I can just imagine Liddy Dole squirreled away in a dark corner of Bowdoin College's Hawthorne-Longfellow Library, drooling over the dust-covered pages of Bowdoin's twenty-year-old newspapers. What I can't figure out is why the press so eagerly slapped this story on the front page of the Rhode Island section, on the day of the final debate no less.

SELLING PAPERS AND SELLING OUT

By the time August 26, 2006, rolled around, the Bowdoin story was merely another piece of shameful journalism in a long line of examples. The more irrelevant a story was to the race, the more eager the press seemed to report on it. By the end of the campaign, I was honestly surprised not to have encountered this headline: "Twelve-Year-Old Laffey and Gang Egged Houses."[2] Instead, the local press occupied themselves with other urgent matters, like my occasional swearing (more on that later) and the pixelation of former Cranston city councilman Randy Jackvony. The pixelation issue was so important that it warranted a front-page above-the-fold Rhode Island section story in the *Providence Journal*, and a total of 630 words (with two big color pictures). In contrast, when I introduced a forty-five-page policy brief on the dire need for reforming the tax code and making the tax cuts permanent, the *Providence Journal* story on that press conference totaled 508 words.

If you're not from Rhode Island, you're probably scratching your head and wondering, *What is pixelation?* That is a valid question, because "pixelation" isn't actually a word according to *Merriam-Webster's Collegiate Dictionary* (eleventh edition). A "Pixel," according to the same dictionary, is defined as "any of the small discrete elements that together constitute an image (as on a television or computer screen)." For example, if you were to blow up a photograph very large, you would find that the photo is made up of individual colored boxes, called pixels. So far so good. In the case of Randy Jackvony, to pixelate is to block out his face and body with small, colored boxes. It is also an excuse to have a good laugh.

Me with a pixelated Jack Vony, Allan Fung, and Robin Schutt.

Randy Jackvony was the chairman of the Cranston Republican Party when I came home from Memphis. As you may recall from Chapter 1, he oversaw the comically unsuccessful meeting that tried to stop me from running for mayor. Jackvony stepped down in 2002 to run for one of Cranston's three at-large city council seats, barely winning that race by 141 votes.

Over the following two years, my relationship with Jackvony—along with my patience—was constantly tested by Jackvony's self-centeredness. Now, I certainly garnered my share of criticism over my four years as mayor, and I will be the first to admit that my blunt style sometimes ticks people off, but ultimately my decisions as mayor were made with the best interests of the taxpayers in mind and were backed up by Cranston's Democratic-controlled city council. Every single one of my four budgets was passed unanimously, with one exception. Yup, you got it: Republican councilman Randy Jackvony. In other words, all the Democrats, including the city council president, who had run against me in my first race, approved my budgets, but not Randy Jackvony. Jackvony couldn't find room in his massive ego to put the Cranston taxpayers ahead of himself. When it came to public service, Jackvony was the kind of guy who'd rather be a general in a phone booth than a captain in a real army.

In 2004, when I was running for reelection for mayor, Jackvony also ran for reelection but was angered when the Cranston Republican Party offered him the second spot on the citywide ballot instead of the coveted first spot. This decision was based on the candidates' performance in the previous election cycle. Given Jackvony's razor-thin margin of victory in 2002, he understandably did not qualify for the first spot. Unable to get his way as an at-large candidate, Jackvony decided to run for city council in Ward 4 even though the Cranston Republican Party already had a candidate. I, along with the rest of the Cranston party, supported the other candidate.[3] In the end, Jackvony lost.

At some point in the summer of 2004, during this whole local hullabaloo, my graphics guy went onto my mayoral campaign Web site and pixelated out Randy Jackvony from the 2002 pictures. A little pink and blue over his hair, a little yellow in the middle . . . Randy Jackvony never looked so good! We all shared a hearty laugh and forgot about the picture, until it showed up on the front page of the Rhode Island section of the *Providence Journal* on December 15, 2005. By then, the picture had been buried in the archived section of my Web site, gathering virtual dust over the past year and a half.

Throughout the campaign, Senator Chafee referred to the pixelation incident as evidence of my alleged instability and combative temperament. During the second radio debate on Rhode Island's WPRO-AM on August 17, 2006, Senator Chafee announced that he had visited my campaign Web site just that morning and found the pixelated picture in the archived section of the photographs. Gasp! Consider the following transcript from the debate and note that the hemming on Chafee's part is *not* exaggerated:

CHAFEE: . . . *Uh, still, this morning, I checked your Web site Mayor Laffey, Councilman Jackvony—still on your Web site uh, with the uh, uh, humiliating, uh, pixelating, which is the computer uh, graphic* [Laffey chuckling] *that humiliating a man still on your Web site, just take the picture down, so, I think it, it is relevant.*

LAFFEY: *Mr. Chafee, you really spent this morning on the archived section of the elect Laffey section, that's what you were doing—going through it?*

CHAFEE: *I wanted to make sure that it was still up. People told me it was still up, and I said show me.*

If this seems odd to you, you're in good company. For one, I found this exchange rather comical, evidenced by my audible chuckle. But don't just take my word for it. At the end of the segment, the host, Dan Yorke, had this to say about Senator Chafee's sense of humor: "The senator, as often happens to the best of comedians, did not get the joke."

In Senator Chafee's eyes, this harmless prank was the ultimate offense. Forget the fact that Senator Chafee doesn't support the death penalty for Osama bin Laden, forget the fact that Senator Chafee didn't want to impose sanctions on terrorist sponsor Syria, and forget the fact that Senator Chafee couldn't remember his own position on illegal immigration when asked on public radio (it's amnesty, by the way). Forget all that, because the pixelation of Randy Jackvony overshadows everything else!

You can't see me right now, but I'm hanging my head in shame. I am guilty as charged. Guilty of leaving the pixelated picture up on my Web site. I am also guilty of instructing my graphics guy to post a little welcome note to the senator, so that when

Linc Chafee checked the archived section of my Web site every morning, he would see these words painted in bright Laffey blue: "Good morning, Mr. Chafee." Yes, I am guilty of all these things. Most of all, I am guilty of having a sense of humor.

But the press is guilty of a much greater crime. It is guilty of gorging itself on stupid, irrelevant issues like the pixelation of Randy Jackvony when there were real differences between Senator Chafee and me worthy of discussion. And they wonder why the stock prices of media companies keep going down.

When it came to giving Senator Chafee a pass, the press was all too eager to oblige, especially with respect to Chafee's outrageous positions on foreign policy. The so-called mainstream press had a habit of calling Senator Chafee a moderate, but when it came to foreign policy issues, Senator Chafee, the third-ranking member of the Senate Committee on Foreign Relations, and a possible member of a Neville Chamberlain fan club,[4] often found himself not a minority among Republicans, but a minority among the entire U.S. Senate. "Moderate" was the understatement of the century, right up there with, "Ahh, Houston, we have a problem."

The most egregious offense was Senator Chafee's vote against imposing sanctions on terrorist sponsor Syria in November 2003. Eighty-seven U.S. senators voted for the Syria Accountability Act; four did not. Linc Chafee was in the latter group. At the time, Chafee defended his vote, saying that he was convinced to vote against sanctions by Turkey's prime minister, Recep Tayyip Erdogan, who argued that Syria is slowly reforming and that if "you give [Syrian president Bashar al-]Assad room and time, he will be more pro-Western than you might think. That was his advice," Chafee added, "and what more can you do than to listen?"

Now, you might think an astounding statement like this one by a sitting U.S. senator could be found in the *New York Times*, the *Washington Post*, or Rhode Island's *Providence Journal*. But no, you'll have to search far and wide to find this alarming admission by Senator Chafee, buried deep in a February 2004 article by reporter Ori Nir in the small Jewish weekly, the *Forward*.

But it gets worse. Three years later, Senator Chafee was still taking his foreign policy advice from Middle Eastern leaders. In July 2006, as Israel struggled to ward off the terrorist group Hezbollah in Lebanon, Senator Chafee brazenly called for a "cease-fire immediately" only days after Hezbollah invaded Israel and kidnapped two of its soldiers. When asked by David Gregory of MSNBC about President Bush's desire to exert pressure on Syria, one of Hezbollah's chief sponsors, Lincoln Chafee responded as follows:

> *Well, the Egyptian foreign minister said that Syria is actually kind of hanging in the balance as to whether they want to go more towards Iran* or actually if you can believe it more towards the west. *We have opportunities and to continually flail at Syria as the root cause of this problem I think is wrong. I think it's the opportunity backed by what the Egyptian foreign minister said yesterday to try and repair assimilations with some of our adversaries, Syria in particular.*

Actually, I *can't* believe it. Syria doesn't exactly inspire that warm and fuzzy feeling. Since 1979, the U.S. State Department has put Syria on its list of state sponsors of terrorism, along with Iran, Iraq, Libya, Cuba, North Korea, and Sudan. According to an April 2006 State Department report, the Syrian government "continued to provide political and material support to both Hezbollah and Palestinian terrorist groups. HAMAS, Palestinian Islamic Jihad (PIJ), the Popular Front for the Liberation of Palestine (PFLP), and the Popular Front for the Liberation of Palestine-General Command (PFLP-GC), among others, base their external leadership in Damascus."

This shocking call for an immediate cease-fire was similarly absent from press reports, as was Chafee's penchant for taking cues from foreign leaders. The press was also mum when Chafee refused to sign a letter, signed by eighty-eight of his Senate colleagues, urging Europe to add Hezbollah to its terrorist list, and thereby denying the terrorist group funding. For anyone concerned about the role that Syria and Iran play in an increasingly violent Middle East, Senator Chafee's appeasement and the press's silence were as outrageous as they were frightening.

Senator Chafee highlighted the pixelation incident as proof of a mean and scary Steve Laffey. But you tell me—what is more frightening? A mayor who engages in a little harmless fun at the expense of a political foe, or a sitting U.S. senator who takes his foreign policy advice from the prime minister of Turkey and the foreign minister of Egypt, and thinks Iran and Syria will become democracies if we just send over our national Ping-Pong team for a little singles and doubles tournament?[5] I have five children whom I worry about every day, so I'm going to say the latter option.

Too often, I heard reporters and columnists complain that the campaign was focused on silly fistfights and not on serious topics, but these critics could have benefited from a hard look in the mirror. Not only did the press print almost every ridiculous accusation regardless of the evidence and relevance to the race, but it was not uncommon for reporters and columnists to pursue and even initiate irrelevant story lines. Nowhere was this more true than when it came to religion.

There are a lot of things the press considers sacred. For example, when Rhode Island congressman Patrick Kennedy drove his car into a security barrier on Capitol Hill, the press fell over itself so as not to overstep the sensitive boundaries of Patrick Kennedy's prescription drug problem. Like I said, there are a lot of things the press considers sacred. Religion is not one of them.

In this age of overcooked political correctness, in which we're all supposed to dance around on our toes so as not to insult anyone, for some unexplained reason it is still okay to plunge into the intricate particulars of a candidate's religious faith. Do you consider yourself Catholic? What church do you go to? You say you grew up Catholic, but you attend a nondenominational church? What religion does your wife practice? And so on. Questions like these are simply not okay. Of course, that doesn't stop the press from asking them.

When I first ran for mayor, a Rhode Island columnist wanted to talk about my religious faith. I explained to him that my faith has always been an important part of my life and is the thing that has kept me going even in some very difficult times. When I came home to Cranston from Memphis, I didn't know what I would do. I thought about starting my own investment banking firm and considered other options, but given the financial disaster that was happening in Cranston, "it just became very clear to me," I told the columnist, "God, you sent me home to run for mayor."

To me, this was a perfectly reasonable expression of my faith. Obviously, I wasn't telling him that God appeared to me à la Moses and the burning bush and told me to run for mayor. As a man of faith, I try to see God's hand in every facet of my life. I try to find meaning in the events and decisions that take place around me. Fixing Cranston was just one of those moments for me.

For others of faith, this will not seem strange at all. But to the liberal intelligentsia—and that is giving them a little too much credit—this was an outrageous thing to say. The above columnist pegged me as a religious fanatic and would, throughout the campaign, pepper me with questions along these lines in search of further evidence. Even the Associated Press latched on to this theory, using this line as proof of my outrageousness: "Republican Senate candidate Stephen P. Laffey once told a newspaper columnist that God wanted him to run for mayor of Cranston."

Let me be clear. Like the vast majority of Americans, I am proud of my religious faith, and I believe it plays an important role in my personal life. But its relevance to cutting taxes and wasteful spending eludes my grasp. Unfortunately, the evidence of real issues worthy of discussion was not enough to deter the press from harping on this matter.

This is not about my wounded feelings. The mainstream media's attitude toward religion and candidates of religious faith borders on hostility and is offensive to millions of Americans. This is not just a question of Republican versus Democrat (though the press does tend to give Democrats a pass when it comes to religion). There are plenty of Democrats who take their faith seriously, and they too should be offended by the liberal media's treatment of religion in the political arena.[6]

Nor do I blame the media for my primary loss. I'm a big boy, and I can take care of myself. But the degeneration of political campaigns into a wrestling match has a corrosive effect on the political process. Throughout the campaign I received phone calls from friends who said things like "This is why I would never run for political office . . . I'm going to live vicariously through you." There are a lot of smart, talented Republicans out there interested in talking about real issues and working to make this country better, but they have no interest in dealing with the mudslinging and the tabloid journalism of the mainstream press.

I was lucky enough to be born with an extra-thick skin and find most of these shenanigans pretty funny, but regular folks with normal skin don't want to subject themselves and their families to this insanity. Indeed, Chafee supporters even went so low as to spin nasty false rumors about my wife on the blog sites. When people hear about these kinds of incidents, they say, "Forget it.

If this is what politics is about, I don't want any part in it." For me, politics was never about who can dig up more dirt about the other person. It was always and will always be about solving real problems.

MONKEYING AROUND

While I was working with my campaign staff to produce detailed policy briefs on the major issues of our time and while Chafee's staff and the NRSC were busy unearthing my childhood pranks, Senator Chafee was working hard in Washington to produce legislation that had little effect on the vast majority of American lives. A quick glance at some key examples of Chafee's sponsored legislation over the past seven years demonstrates that this is true:

- **S.RES.301:** A resolution commemorating the one-hundredth anniversary of the National Audubon Society.

- **S.3240:** A bill to amend the Harmonized Tariff Schedule of the United States to clarify the tariff treatment of textile parts of seats and other furniture.

- **S.RES.365:** A resolution congratulating the people of Brazil on the completion of peaceful, free, and fair elections in Brazil and the election of President Luiz Inácio Lula da Silva.

- **S.2033:** A bill to authorize appropriations for the John H. Chafee Blackstone River Valley National Heritage Corridor in Massachusetts and Rhode Island, and for other purposes.

- **S.AMDT.3545 to S.2522:** To express the sense of the Senate that the United States should authorize and fully fund a bilateral and multilateral program of debt relief for the world's poorest countries.

This is not to say that the sentiments behind some of these bills are not laudable—just don't get me started on the practice of lending taxpayer dollars to corrupt foreign countries, knowing up front they will never repay the debt. I'm all for congratulating Brazil on fair elections, but it would have been nice if Chafee had something a little more substantial to show for his seven years in the U.S. Senate. You might think that I went through Chafee's sponsored legislation and specifically chose the more insignificant examples, but no. Feel free to do the search yourself at http://thomas.loc.gov. You'll find what I found: not much. Given his uninspiring record, it is not hard to imagine why the private research firm Knowlegis (www.knowlegis.net) rated Chafee the ninety-fifth most influential senator in the entire U.S. Senate, and the fifty-fifth out of fifty-five Republicans.

Even Senator Chafee was at a loss to articulate legislation he was proud of. In a post-election episode of *The Daily Show*, host Jon Stewart asked Chafee, "Can you point to anything in the last five years you think Congress should be proud of?" Chafee's response: "Uh . . . I better come up with something before I leave here . . . I'll come up with it." When I heard this, a lot of thoughts flew through my brain, but Jon Stewart summed up my thoughts better than I could with this one-liner: "It was the saddest thing I ever saw."

Of all the bills Chafee sponsored, the one that most demonstrates his irrelevancy is S.1509, or the Captive Primate Safety Act, which according to a press release from Chafee's Senate office, "adds nonhuman primates to the list of animals that cannot be transported across state lines for pet trade. This includes chimpanzees, monkeys, baboons, and other primates." You hear that, monkey owners of America? Chafee thinks you're dangerous. If you own a gorilla, keep it in Kansas. I can only assume Chafee dreamed up this urgent legislation after catching either one of Clint Eastwood's only bad movies, *Any Which Way but Loose* (1978) and *Any Which Way You Can* (1980).

In all fairness, Chafee claimed there was a dire need for legislation of this sort. Over the past decade, one hundred people have been injured by primates, according to the Captive Wild Animal Protection Coalition. That's ten people per year, or 0.000003 percent of the American population.

This kind of legislation highlights the major problem with Senator Chafee's seven-year record in the U.S. Senate: he didn't have one, or at least not a very impressive one. For many Republicans, Senator Chafee's liberal positions were more than enough reason to vote him out of office. For others, his inefficacy and his follower status made him, not so much a thorn in their side, but an embarrassment. Throughout the race, reporters asked me if Chafee was a Republican In Name Only (RINO). Of course that ranks as one of the more absurd questions I received on the campaign trail. A doorknob could tell you that Chafee was a RINO, but that's not the real reason I ran. I ran because there were real problems in this country, and Chafee didn't have the guts or capacity to take hold of the reins and lead.

Throughout the race, my staffers summed up the problem with Senator Chafee's record with one line: "It's not enough just to vote on stuff." Being a U.S. senator means being a leader. It means doing things instead of just saying things, it means persuading colleagues when you think they're wrong, and sometimes it means rocking the boat. Senator Chafee was a lot of things, but he was not a doer, he was not a persuader, and he was not a rocker of boats. Senator Chafee was not a leader.

When it came time for me to give my closing statement in my first televised debate with Senator Chafee, I eschewed my typewritten speech, looked directly into the camera, and told the American people exactly what I thought a U.S. senator should be:

> *I know that if you put me down in Washington, one thing I will not be is irrelevant. I will fight every single day for the taxpayers of America and the taxpayers of Rhode Island to right the ship. We are in the wrong direction, folks. And it's just like this: If you think down in Washington, everything is okay and you want some people just to be sitting in the stand eating a couple of hot dogs watching the game, vote for one of the other two guys. But if you want somebody to get on the mound and throw some fastballs and take on the enemy and protect the teammates—that['s] you the taxpayers, then you want me. Thank you. God bless and thank you for having me here tonight.*

If you are wondering why the National Republican Senatorial Committee never once ran an ad in Rhode Island promoting Lincoln Chafee (as you will soon see in the next chapter) or why the NRSC's entire Rhode Island strategy was based on destroying my character, you need not look further than Chafee's vaunted monkey bill. Put simply, there was nothing positive for the NRSC to say.

CHAPTER 6

Ads, Ads, and Lies

"Blaine, Blaine, James G. Blaine, the Continental Liar from the State of Maine."–Grover Cleveland supporters, 1884

RATIONALIZING THE IRRATIONAL

Negative ads in tightly contested political races are nothing new. Every two years, the media writes another story claiming, "unprecedented negativity," but low-down negative campaigning goes back all the way to the 1800 presidential campaign, during which the anti-Jefferson camp labeled the Founding Father "a mean-spirited, low-lived fellow, the son of a half-breed Indian squaw, sired by a Virginia mulatto father." Modern campaign commercials accuse opponents of sporting bad haircuts and engaging in Playboy romps, but these personal attacks are not all that different from some older versions. In the 1884 presidential election, supporters of James G. Blaine accused Grover Cleveland of fathering an illegitimate child, amusing themselves with this chant: "Ma, Ma, where's my pa? Gone to the White House, ha ha ha!"

The ads the NRSC ran against me did not quite rise to the level of "illegitimate children." To be sure, the NRSC ads were vicious and false, but that was not even the worst part about them. In an unprecedented move, these negative ads came from the Republican Party itself. As I pointed out in Chapter 1, the Republican Party had never before engaged in negative ads against another member of its own party, let alone a relatively conservative Republican in favor of a shamefully liberal one.

The rationale for the NRSC's nasty campaign was a classic realpolitik justification: Lincoln Chafee "is the only Republican that can keep this seat for our party and will prevent the seat from falling into the hands of a liberal Democrat," said NRSC spokesman Dan Ronayne. Throughout the race, this line of reasoning was summed up by one word: electability. Next to "Vote for me because my last name is Chafee," electability became the rallying cry of the Chafee campaign: "Vote for me because I'm the best you can do."

The NRSC first touched on this line of reasoning when Mark Stephens called me in the summer of 2005 to relay the results of the push poll the NRSC had commissioned, but the same line would be parroted throughout the entire campaign. A year later, the NRSC sounded the same tune, releasing this statement five days before the primary: "Polls and common sense have said all along Steve Laffey is unelectable in a general election and he faces long odds of beating Lincoln Chafee in the Republican primary. Lincoln Chafee will win the primary, and is the only Republican who can beat Sheldon Whitehouse in the general."

The NRSC's statement could have been taken straight out of the pages of Gerald Ford's 1976 playbook, as detailed by Craig Shirley in his book, *Reagan's Revolution*. Thirty years earlier, when Reagan announced his candidacy for the presidency in November 1975, President Ford's campaign released a statement that sounds uncannily like the NRSC's 2006 version: "Despite how well

Ronald Reagan does or does not do in the early primaries, the simple political fact is that he cannot defeat any candidate the Democrats put up. Reagan's constituency is much too narrow, even within the Republican Party." This sentiment was echoed by a host of party players like Senator Chuck Percy of Illinois, who labeled Reagan "far out of the centrist stream" and warned that "a Reagan nomination, and the crushing defeat likely to follow, could signal the beginning of the end of our party as an effective force in American life."

Thirty years after the Republican establishment backed the "electable" guy and the United States ended up with Jimmy Carter as president, I asked myself: Has the Republican Party learned anything over the past three decades? As I listened to NRSC communications director Brian Nick vowing not to support my candidacy if I won the primary, I knew the answer was no. "We are not going to spend any resources on somebody who has no chance of winning," Nick said. "It would be silly to do so." This was perfectly okay with me. I told a reporter for the *Weekly Standard* to pass on the following message: "Stay the heck out of Rhode Island. The last thing that Karl Rove and his buddies want in Washington is a real reformer like myself."

Historical precedent aside, there were several glitches in the electability argument. The most striking problem was that "the best you can do" turned out to be pretty shoddy. On all the important issues Senator Chafee voted with the Democrats, and on foreign policy issues he was often found wandering on the far left end of the Senate bell curve. Perhaps this explains Chafee's score of 12 from the American Conservative Union, the same as Hillary Clinton's score and one point below that of Wisconsin senator Russ Feingold, Chafee's "Let's censor the President" friend.

Second, Rhode Island has a history of electing candidates who have conservative views on many issues, including the current conservative governor, Don Carcieri, who is pro-life. Democratic U.S. representative Jim Langevin is also pro-life, as is the speaker of the state House of Representatives, the president of the state Senate, and the secretary of state–all Democrats.

But the greatest problem with the electability argument was that it was quickly punctured by reality. From the very beginning Chafee struggled to get his poll numbers above 45 percent, and only a couple of days after the primary, Chafee's already low numbers started sinking fast. Suddenly, the NRSC's negative ads, which had been ubiquitous during the primary race, were nowhere to be seen. With more important Senate seats falling into danger around the country, the NRSC cut its losses in Rhode Island, making a public mockery of its electability claims. Come November 7, Chafee was defeated by his Democratic opponent, Sheldon Whitehouse. And Republicans around the state, still fuming at the NRSC's great betrayal, wondered: What the heck happened to electability?

REAPING WHAT YOU SOW

Ultimately, Chafee was the one with the electability problem because he had nothing to offer voters in Rhode Island. As I delineated in an early ad, Linc Chafee and his Democratic opponent, Sheldon Whitehouse, were two peas in a pod, right down to their patrician roots, inherited money, and fathers who were roommates at Yale University. For more on their striking similarities, see Table 6.1.

Thus, voters had a choice between a real Democrat and a fake Democrat. Club for Growth president Pat Toomey wrote in a post-election op-ed that, "as they usually will, voters choose the real thing instead of the faux politician." Toomey also wrote, "I still think the anti-Washington, anti-establishment, populist

TABLE 6.1 TWO PEAS IN A POD

ISSUE	LINCOLN CHAFEE (R)	SHELDON WHITEHOUSE (D)
Taxes	Voted against every single Bush tax cut.	"We need to repeal the Bush tax cuts."
Estate tax	Voted against repeal. Said, "The rich are a useful source of revenue."	Opposes repeal.
Happy the Democrats took control of Congress	Yes.	Yes.
Judge Samuel Alito	Was the only Republican to vote against Alito's nomination.	Opposed Alito and supported the filibuster against his nomination.
Illegal immigration	Supports amnesty.	Supports amnesty.
Flag burning	Voted against protecting the flag twice. The second time, Chafee cast the deciding vote against protecting our flag.	Against amendment protecting the flag.
Voted for George W. Bush	No.	No.
Censure the president	Called it a "positive" thing.	Said President Bush "merit[ed] censure."
Abortion	Abortion on demand.	Abortion on demand.
Gay marriage	Supports.	Supports.
Iraq War.	Still trying to figure out his position.	Supports a rapid and responsible withdrawal of our troops from Iraq.
School choice	Against.	Against.
No Child Left Behind	Voted for NCLB.	Supports fully funding NCLB; received the NEA's endorsement.

Laffey would have had at least as good a chance, especially in this election's anti-incumbent environment, as the ultimate establishment, pseudo-Democrat Chafee."

As the sun set on primary day, Senator Chafee was busy celebrating his win, but all the NRSC had to show for itself was a throng of angry Republicans across America and a portfolio of embarrassing ads. Back in the spring of 2005, the national Republican Party made a strategic decision to pursue power over principle and let the chips fall where they may. As Chafee went down in defeat on November 7, they had neither principle nor power to show for their efforts. And the reason is that power is not a very convincing message.

In the Rhode Island primary, the national Republican Party, given its enormous resources, was able to persuade enough liberal Democrats and Independents to come out to vote for Lincoln Chafee but never once attempted to articulate a persuasive message for why Senator Chafee was worthy of occupying the historic halls of the U.S. Senate. Remember my first meeting with Elizabeth Dole?–"We're not here to defend Linc Chafee." Not exactly a "shining city on a hill" speech. Nor did the party articulate a convincing message for why Republicans should maintain a majority. Instead, all its energies and money were focused on persuading voters that I was not fit for the U.S. Senate. But once Liddy Dole accomplished her goal of defeating me, she and her buddies were back to square one, and now they were facing a Democrat in a political environment that was more favorable to Democrats than to Republicans.

Chafee himself suffered from the same problem. He spent the whole primary campaigning on electability and attacking my character, but with me out of the race, what did Linc Chafee have to offer the electorate? Just the Chafee name and a history of negative ads, eviscerating his only saving grace–his erstwhile reputation for being a "nice guy." The Chafee campaign spent $3.2

million to defeat me, and the Republican Party chipped in with upward of another $2 million. They defeated me all right, but they didn't win. They didn't win in Rhode Island, and they didn't win around the country.

LYING THROUGH ITS TEETH

The NRSC used every weapon at its disposal to defeat me, including negative ads, automated phone messages, and piles and piles of attack mailers. I know, because I received every one of them. The advantage of mailers is that you can get away with more than you can on television, because they are somewhat shielded from the scrutiny of the press. In other words, it is easier to lie. Mailers are also cheaper and can be targeted to specific audiences, though it never occurred to the geniuses at the NRSC to take the Laffey family off its list. Needless to say, my wife was awfully surprised to take in the mail each day and discover all the horrible crimes I had committed unbeknownst to her. Who was this villain she had married twelve years ago?

My wife learned all sorts of new and interesting tidbits about my life. Apparently, I recklessly spent taxpayer dollars even though the *Providence Journal* documented all the spending cuts I made as mayor and the fierce battles I fought to make those cuts. According to the same impeccable sources, I also "scratched the back of a big company by giving them a no-bid contract" and "kept it secret from the public," though the trial "bid" in question totaled an astonishing $10, and the entire Rhode Island press corps was present at the May 2005 press conference in which I unveiled this "secret bid." She discovered that I abandoned injured firemen, had a "history of operating in the back room," and moonlighted as a bare-chested disco dancer. After all that, I'm lucky my wife didn't pick up and move back to Memphis.

When it came to tearing me apart, the NRSC displayed no

shame. But worse than all the stupid, irrelevant accusations—did I mention my mayor's car had a leather interior?—was its attempt to disqualify my Republican credentials. Thus, I found myself in the most unusual predicament. From the mainstream press, I was described as too right for the liberal bastion of Rhode Island,[1] and from the Republican national establishment as not conservative enough!

The NRSC called me "just another tax-and-spend politician," though it was Chafee who voted for the Bridge to Nowhere *twice* and boasted about voting against every single Bush tax cut.

NEWSWEEK: *In the past you've taken some heat from your own party, essentially for not being "Republican enough." You voted against Alito, against the Iraq war—even against the president himself in 2004.*

LINCOLN CHAFEE: *And his tax cuts. Don't forget that.*

The NRSC and Chafee campaign both accused me of being weak on immigration even though Chafee was the only Republican in the Senate to vote for amnesty for all twelve million illegal aliens. And the NRSC accused me of being weak on national security even though it was Chafee who opposed the death penalty for Osama bin Laden, as he so eloquently explained during our last debate:

NBC's JIM TARICANI: *Senator, if Osama bin Laden is captured, tried, and found guilty in a U.S. court of masterminding the 9/11 attacks, federal prosecutors will have the option to ask for the death penalty. Would you support the death penalty for bin Laden?*

CHAFEE: *Highly emotional issue, uh, but Rhode Island executed an innocent man, uh, in the nineteenth century and I oppose the death penalty.*

TARICANI: *My question is premised on the fact that Mr. bin Laden would be found guilty.*

CHAFEE: *Yes, yes, uh, I found—I oppose the death penalty. Some highly emotional issues will come up and you've probably mentioned the most highly emotional of all—bin Laden responsible for all the mayhem on September 11.*

But nothing was more shocking than a mailer adorned with an unflattering picture of Hillary Clinton, circa 1994, that arrived at my doorstep the Thursday before primary day. In bold white letters, the mailer read: "Who called Hillary Clinton's position 'reasonable?'" Turn over the mailer to find the answer: "Steve Laffey said Hillary Clinton has 'reasonable' views on abortion." The mailer goes on to list Clinton's egregious positions, including her support for partial-birth abortion and her opposition to parental notification laws.

Clearly, the intention of this mailer was to keep pro-life voters away from the polls, an important factor given the large number of pro-life voters in Rhode Island. My pro-life positions, however, were well documented and well within the mainstream. If anyone was extreme on abortion it was Linc Chafee, endorsed by the likes of the National Abortion Rights Action League (NARAL) and Planned Parenthood, a distinction usually reserved for the most left-wing Democrats. Indeed, many left-wingers kicked and screamed when the abortion groups bestowed their endorsements and PAC checks on the Republican Chafee, but the groups were quick to defend their favorite Republican. Senator Chafee's eager support for partial birth abortion, his opposition to Laci's Law and parental notification, and his refusal to vote for any judge who didn't promise to uphold *Roe v. Wade* earned him high marks from abortion-rights groups. I guess when you're that extreme it doesn't matter whether you call yourself a Democrat or a Republican.

The truth behind this mailer was not all that complicated, though apparently too complicated for the likes of the NRSC. In January 2005, Hillary Clinton gave a speech that caused ripples among the press, in which she called abortion a "tragic choice" and spoke about reducing the number of abortions in this country. I don't agree with Hillary Clinton on most things, but I do agree that every abortion is a tragedy, and I wish that more people in the Democratic Party would have the guts to stand up and say the same thing. Pro-choice or pro-life, most Americans agree that the extinguishing of life or potential life is nothing to smile about. That's all I meant when I called that particular comment reasonable. I meant that it was a drastic improvement over groups like NARAL that view abortion as a badge of pride and extremists who sell T-shirts proudly proclaiming: "I had an abortion."[2]

The painful irony was that this mailer was sent in defense of a senator who received a 100 percent rating from NARAL. It was sent in defense of a senator who would do everything in his power to undermine the very values the mailer purported to support.

Nationally, Liddy Dole pretended to fight for Republican principles. In fund-raising appeals sent to Republicans across the country, she warned, "What would a Democratic majority mean for you and me? It would mean President Bush's tax cuts would expire, conservative federal judges would be rejected in favor of liberal activist judges, cut-and-run foreign policies would cost us the War on Terrorism." But Liddy Dole didn't bother to explain in this letter why the Republican Party was spending upward of $2 million to support a senator who, if reelected, would work to enact the policies Dole warned against. After all, it was Chafee who voted against Bush's tax cuts, and it was Chafee who wanted "liberal activist judges." Liddy Dole wanted to have it both ways.

She wanted the Republican base to come out in droves in Virginia, Montana, Pennsylvania, and Tennessee, but she wanted the same Republican base to stay home in Rhode Island. Her problem: she thought the American people were stupid. Turns out, we're pretty darn smart.

Had I wanted to get down in the mud with the Chafee campaign and the NRSC, I had plenty of information at my disposal. I could have run ads with clips of Chafee admitting to using cocaine in college, or clips of Chafee working illegally in Canada shoeing horses. Imagine this creative ad on Rhode Island's major TV stations:

> *Linc Chafee is throwing mud at Steve Laffey because he is afraid of the truth. The truth? Linc Chafee is a confessed cocaine abuser. The truth? Linc Chafee was an illegal alien himself. Can we trust a cocaine abuser to protect our children? Can we trust an illegal alien to protect our borders? The answer? No.*

But that's not what this race was about. It wasn't about sliming the other guy or deciding who was more outrageous when we were twenty years old. This race, at least from my end, was about who had a better track record of success and who had a more compelling vision for the future.

Throughout the campaign, Chafee claimed that his commercials were not negative ads but contrast ads that pointed out the differences between his record and my own. I don't have a problem with contrast ads. In an early ad, I pointed out that Senator Chafee and the Democratic candidate, Sheldon Whitehouse, were really two peas in a pod—which would be later confirmed in the general election when a panelist in Chafee's first televised debate with Whitehouse asked Linc what distinguished him from the Democrats, and Chafee stuttered and stammered about the tradition of moderate northeastern Republicans. The Club for Growth also ran ads attacking Senator Chafee for opposing tax cuts and supporting wasteful pork-barrel projects. These claims were legitimate, completely truthful, and publicly confirmed by Chafee himself.

What I object to—and what we should all object to—are outright lies and character assassination. Even Senator Chafee himself admitted three days before the primary that his ads were unfair, "saying he dislike[d] one that criticizes Laffey for raising taxes when Cranston was near bankruptcy," according to the Associated Press. "Most voters think Laffey had to do it," Chafee said.

The NRSC, too, came to appreciate the depth of its betrayal. As I was writing this chapter, I went to the NRSC's Web site to review the negative ads it had aired against me. I found Chafee's "I'm so wonderful" ads and the single commercial the NRSC ran against Sheldon Whitehouse, but the heaps of money wasted on attacking my character were nowhere to be seen. In contrast, a quick search of any other state with a competitive race—Tennessee, Montana, Pennsylvania, Ohio, Virginia, Maryland, Missouri, and New Jersey—provided a smorgasbord of negative NRSC ads run against Democrats in each of those states. I found out that Harold Ford partied with Playboy playmates in lingerie and Jon Tester voted against protecting our kids, but where were all the inventive lies the NRSC told about me? Liddy Dole may have persuaded herself of the Machiavellian virtue of her betrayal, but clearly someone at the NRSC realized that publicizing its knife-in-the-back routine was not the smartest idea.

That's where Chafee and the NRSC went wrong. They thought they could jettison principle on the campaign trail in the name of winning and, at the same time, tell the country to vote for Republicans so that they could fight for principle and integrity. Chafee himself spent $150,000 worth of television ad time pledging to "restore a climate of civility, decency, and hope back to our country," but had no compunction about sullying my record and my character with lies. I don't know about you, but I'm still trying to figure out how that qualifies as civil, decent, or hopeful. The Washington Republicans convinced themselves that the ends justified the means, but here's another way to look at it: maybe the means caused the ends.

NOTHING LIKE REAGAN

Ultimately, Liddy Dole's biggest mistake was that she actually bought her own spin. She honestly believed that Chafee was the best the Republican Party could do in Rhode Island, even though the conservative Reagan won Rhode Island in 1984. To be sure, the differences between Ronald Reagan and the national party today (as evidenced by Liddy Dole's leadership) are too long to list, but one major difference deserves mentioning. Reagan actually believed in the ideas he spoke about, and he believed in the universal value of those ideas. After all, it was Reagan who said:

> *I wasn't a great communicator, but I communicated great things, and they didn't spring full bloom from my brow, they came from the heart of a great nation—from our experience, our wisdom, and our belief in principles that have guided us for two centuries. They called it the Reagan revolution. Well, I'll accept that, but for me it always seemed more like the great rediscovery, a rediscovery of our values and our common sense.*

Reagan didn't think that he had to compromise on his ideals in order to win votes, because he believed that the ideals themselves were great ones. And he didn't win Rhode Island in 1984 because he acted like a Democrat; he won because he was true to himself. Reagan didn't talk about tax cuts in South Carolina and tax hikes in Rhode Island. He knew he didn't have to. All he had to do was tell people the truth. If he explained to them how the economy worked, if he explained to them the nature of the Communist enemy we were dealing with, he believed—rightly—that people would listen, and they would understand.

Reagan believed that hardworking Americans—no matter where they lived and no matter what their party affiliation—wanted to control their own lives and live securely and in freedom. Reagan was called a lot of things by a lot of people, but he was, at heart, an optimist who had tremendous faith in the American people.

Liddy Dole didn't share Reagan's optimism, and she certainly didn't share his faith. She believed that the Republican Party had to settle for Linc Chafee, because she believed voters in Rhode Island were willing to settle. She was no different from the establishment figures who thought Reagan couldn't win in 1976 and 1980 and rejected the former governor as likely to produce "a Goldwater-type disaster." Reagan never believed that. He knew he could win, not because of who he was, but because of what he stood for.

In a column in October 2005, Ann Coulter explained that Reagan's greatness lay in his interaction with regular Americans. Reagan, she wrote,

> *didn't need a bunch of high-priced Bob Shrums to tell him what Americans thought. He knew because of his work with General Electric, touring the country and meeting real Americans. Two months a year for eight years, Reagan would give up to twenty-five speeches a day at G.E. plants, a "marination in middle America," as one G.E. man put it. Reagan himself said, "I always thought Hollywood had the wrong idea of the average American, and the*

G.E. tours proved I was right." Because of these tours, Reagan knew as he calmly told fretful advisers after the Grenada invasion, "You can always trust Americans."

Liddy Dole didn't trust America, and she sure as heck didn't trust Republicans.

CHAPTER 7

Working Our Tails Off—
Rhode Island Style

"C'mon! We're all going to die, die standing up!"–Jed Eckert, while handing out guns to freed Americans, Red Dawn, 1984

LOOKING FOR VOTERS IN THE SNOW

From the very beginning of this race, I was labeled an underdog even by friendly publications like the *National Review.* Though Mark Stephens had informed me that the national Republican Party wouldn't be with me, I didn't know what that meant exactly until the NRSC ran its first ad attacking me for making money in the private sector. After all, the national party had never attacked another Republican before. I was in uncharted territory. Sure, I knew the race would be tough, but it wasn't until that moment that I realized just what kind of Goliath I was up against. So I did what any guy fighting the fight of his life would do: I pulled out every slingshot I had in my pocket, and then some.

Luckily, I live in Rhode Island, where the underground campaign can make a difference. In the spring and summer, this meant a massive grassroots effort to meet every primary voter in the tiny state of Rhode Island (see Chapter 8), but during New England's brutal winters, knocking on doors and standing in front of Stop & Shops shaking hands wasn't much of an option.

So I did the next best thing. I went on every radio and television show I could; I appeared on shows with national conservative stalwarts like Laura Ingraham and Tony Snow; on Rhode Island's two major talk radio stations, 630 and 920 AM; and on some smaller, less conventional shows. Even the self-professed liberal hosts in Rhode Island welcomed my appearances for the simple reason that I was willing to come on and I made for good radio. In contrast, Chafee, who lived in fear (for good reason) of reminding people that he wasn't his father, was rarely heard over Rhode Island's airwaves. One summer morning, local radio host Dave Barber even used an hour's worth of his morning show to ask the most important question of all: "Where is Senator Chafee?"

I, on the other hand, have loved radio ever since my college days when I hosted *The Joe Show* at Bowdoin College with my buddy Tom Marcelle. Back then we dealt with such fascinating topics as the daily Muffin Report—which consisted of me running downstairs to the cafeteria, grabbing a muffin, running back up, stuffing said muffin in my face, while I reported on the taste and texture of the day's muffin—or the One in a Million Contest, in which I announced that I'd give $1 million to anyone who could guess the number in my head between one and a million. Often I'd yell out: "I got lots of calls for 362,568; I just want everyone to know—that's not the number!" Shockingly, no one ever won.

But the enjoyment and exposure I received were just part of my motivation. More important, I felt a responsibility as a public official to make myself available to the people of Rhode Island. Politicians like to present themselves as public servants, but then the public deserves the opportunity to hold them accountable. Public servants shouldn't hide under their desks or behind their press secretaries because they're uncomfortable with a topic or didn't have the time to memorize their talking points.

So I went basically wherever I was invited and wherever there were listeners, or even a listener. While mainstream radio talk shows in Rhode Island average about ten to fifteen thousand listeners at a given time, some of the smaller, more eclectic stations probably don't even hit the one-thousand mark.

One of my biggest supporters hosted an evening show on WNRI, northern Rhode Island's premier radio station, called *File This with Phil Anez*. Phil is a true grassroots Republican and overall great guy. There may have been five hundred folks listening on the Monday nights I appeared on his show, but how else could I reach five hundred people on a Monday evening in the middle of the winter? Besides, every show began with this caveat: "We called Senator Chafee's office and invited him to come on, but he wasn't interested." For a while, *File This* became the Laffey hour, which was perfectly okay with me.

Another favorite underground radio show was Brian Bishop's *Rule Free Radio*. I had met Brian four years earlier when I ran for mayor. He is your classic working-class, grassroots libertarian who just wants the government to keep its paws off his stuff. He also harbored a love for radio and a unique ability to wax poetic on pretty much anything.

Every Friday night, Brian hosted his own show on local AM radio from the inside of a downtown Providence pub called McFadden's. The interesting thing, at least with respect to my race, was that Brian's show preceded the minor league Providence Bruins hockey game. Fifteen minutes before the pregame show began, five Rhode Island stations tied in to Brian's show. Five radio stations at the same time? I had to be there!

McFadden's was everything a pub should be during Happy Hour on a Friday evening in the middle of February, and everything a normal radio show shouldn't: loud and alcohol infested. As the host, Brian had his own microphone, but the rest of the participating gang had to share a second mike, making orderly discourse something of a challenge. The topics were chosen by Brian and always eclectic. These included tax incremental financing and the 2006 Academy Awards.

The Friday in March following the Academy Awards, Brian sent an e-mail informing me of the week's topic: "Pop culture gets its annual outing tonight as we knock about the Oscars at McFadden's." Since I hadn't actually seen any of the movies nominated for best picture and had no intention of doing so, I knew I needed to brush up on my film credentials.

I put Solly to work. She gave me a look—really more of an icy stare—but she put aside her opposition research and press release of the day and dug into the intricacies of Keira Knightley's eggplant taffeta Vera Wang dress and Reese Witherspoon's performance in *Walk the Line*, loading me up with a stack of papers on those critical issues and more before she disappeared with the Friday-night sun. Now I have no problem rattling off stock symbols and earnings estimates, but my capacity for memorizing Hollywood trivia is comparably less impressive. By the time I was seated at McFadden's listening to Brian talk about the Best Actor nominees, I couldn't remember a stitch of Solly's painstaking research. But I felt the need to contribute, so I blurted out, "You know, I wasn't really into any of the movies this year, but you know that 1984 movie . . . *Red Dawn*, that was a heck of a movie—yeah, *Red Dawn*.[1] I'm kind of shocked it never won an Academy Award!"

With a straight face that probably required a yeoman's self-control, Brian nodded, adding that this B-level movie was "an underrated cult classic" that all conservatives love because of the accurate portrayal of the Evil Empire. Not chagrined in the slightest by my woeful knowledge in the film department, I yelled into the mike, "Wolverine!"—a salute to all *Red Dawn* fans listening to *Rule Free Radio*. I may have sounded like a buffoon to the movie-savvy crowd around me, but to the hockey-loving folks who caught the end of *Rule Free Radio* right before it switched over to the

On September 8, 2005, I announced I was running for the United States Senate. Lincoln Chafee occupied the seat, but he was the most liberal Republican in the Senate and not strong enough to defeat the Democratic candidate, Sheldon Whitehouse.

I grew up in Cranston, and my wife, Kelly, and I are raising our children there. Three of them—Jessie (in my arms), Sarah, and Sam are pictured here.

Republican National Committee Chairman Ken Mehlman (left) called me in early 2005 to talk me out of running for the Senate against Lincoln Chafee. When he failed to convince me, Karl Rove (right) had his deputy telephone me to press the case.

A few months later, Elizabeth Dole summoned me to Washington to meet with her at the National Republican Senatorial Committee, which she chaired in 2006. She tried to talk me into running for Lieutenant Governor instead of for Senate. I told her that if I ran for the Senate, it would be on the great issues of our time. Her executive director replied, "I understand, but we won't be with you."

Just before my last debate against Chafee, an "anonymous" tipster sent a package of my newspaper columns for the Bowdoin Patriot *to the Rhode Island media. I can just imagine Liddy Dole squirreled away in a dark corner of Bowdoin College's Hawthorne-Longfellow Library, drooling over the dust-covered pages of Bowdoin's twenty-year-old newspapers.*

Though he called himself a Republican, Lincoln Chafee opposed Republicans every chance he got. Here he is backslapping Samuel Alito just before he voted against his nomination to the U.S. Supreme Court. Chafee was the only Republican in the Senate to vote against Alito's confirmation, yet the Republican machine in Washington went to bat for him.

In January of 2005, Hillary Clinton gave a speech that caused ripples among the press, in which she called abortion a "tragic choice" and spoke about reducing the number of abortions in this country. That's what I was referring to when I used the word "reasonable." My pro-life positions are well documented and well within the mainstream. And yet this mailer was sent by the National Republican Senatorial Committee in defense of Lincoln Chafee, a senator who received a 100% rating from the National Abortion Rights Action League.

Laura Bush's visit to Rhode Island to campaign and fundraise for Senator Chafee was one of the great ironies of this race. It was also one of the great betrayals. In 1999, Chafee helped whip up the media witchhunt closing in on Bush's alleged cocaine use, and in 2004, Chafee told the press he couldn't bring himself to vote for the President.

John McCain was one of the Washington big-shots who came to Rhode Island to prop up Chafee's dismal campaign. Chafee aired McCain's endorsement speech in ads broadcast around the state. If McCain had any chance of winning the Republican base in the 2008 presidential election, he lost it in Rhode Island.

The Laffey campaign didn't let the Washington attack machine stop us. I pounded on more doors than I could count. Here I am on the move, with volunteers Jackie, Steph, and Eddie. We received a ton of attention from the national media, too. (John Miller of the National Review, who covered my campaign, is also featured in this photo.)

KELLY LAFFEY

Believe it or not, these are not my opponents. Making new friends at the Providence Purim Parade.

KELLY LAFFEY

JOE TATULLI

My three campaign managers: Paul Zisserson ran my mayoral campaigns; John Dodenhoff (right) ran the Senate campaign; Audrey Laffey runs everything else.

Solly yelling at Channel 10 reporter Bill Rappleye. Don't worry; he deserved it.

JOE TATULLI

Harry the Greek guards the Rhody Reformer. When it came to parking the RV, Rule #6 was the most important: Always park the RV with plenty of space around it, so the massive signs on it were visible to voters, and so that we could make a fast get-away if we needed.

Sam and Sarah join me as I march in the Gaspee Day Parade. Come primary day, reporters from around the country were sticking microphones in my face, peppering me with questions about turnout and the NRSC's dirty attack ads, but one local journalist desperately needed to know why my ten-year-old son likes to wear military fatigues. The answer, of course, was: He's ten years old.

Potty training on the campaign trail. With five kids, you do what you have to do.

pregame show, this was like throwing red meat to hungry dogs. No poll would ever tell me if I had changed anybody's mind that night, but I bet one guy out there said, "Any friend of the Wolverines is a friend of mine."

My other major contribution of the night was to announce that Kevin Costner's *Waterworld*, panned by critics everywhere, was actually a pretty darn good movie. I could just see the wheels in Brian's head turning: *This is the last time we invite Mayor Laffey to talk about movies. We'll just stick to the U.S. Senate race.*

HARD CIDER AND THE JUNK MAN

There's a lot of talk about the role of the blogosphere in the political arena. No doubt, certain major blogs play a critical role in disseminating information and holding the mainstream media accountable. Many may recall the excellent work of Little Green Footballs and Power Line in uncovering Dan Rather's fabricated document about President Bush's service in Vietnam. In the same vein, certain liberal blogs successfully assail Republicans, as was the case with George Allen and the "macaca" debacle.

But in the Union's smallest state, where all politics is local, it's a slightly different story. To be sure, the blogs in Rhode Island played a major role in this campaign, just not the role they thought.

There are two major Rhode Island blogs that deal with local politics: Rhode Island's Future (www.rifuture.org), representing the Democratic/liberal wing, and Anchor Rising (www.anchorrising. com), its Republican/conservative/libertarian counterpart. Every once in a blue moon, one of these blogs posts a scoop, but the true role of the Rhode Island blogs is to serve as an outlet for political aggression, especially in the winter months when the weather puts a damper on door-to-door campaigning.

But unlike knocking on doors, the blog wars between the Laffey and Chafee camps was not really about the votes. After all, it was a relatively small group of insiders and politicos who followed the daily posts and comments. No, blogging was a New Age form of psychological warfare and, as a fringe benefit, an immensely enjoyable form of entertainment. See, the key to winning the blog wars came down to two things: organization and a robust sense of humor. No problem there. The Laffey camp excelled at both.

As far as organization went, nothing topped our finely tuned blogging machine in the form of "blog alerts." Every time a post went up on one of the blogs relating to the race, a local Laffey lover took it upon himself to send an e-mail around to a group of trusted supporters with instructions to inundate the blogosphere with the Laffey message. Ranging from levels 1 through 5, a typical e-mail went like this: "Blog Alert Level 5: Chafee is voting against Alito. Go to town!" or "Blog Alert Level 5: On Anchor Rising, there is a post basically condemning the Chafee personal attack ads ... Chafee is losing badly to run these kind of ads." The level of the alert would depend on the urgency of the particular post. Interestingly, blog alerts never dipped below level 3.

To keep the blogs lively—the Laffey camp had very high standards when it came to entertainment—we adopted themes. These themes usually went in cycles. At the beginning, many pro-Laffey bloggers adopted pseudonyms from famous characters most likely to be found on Nickelodeon's channel TV Land, like the dedicated blogger Fred Sanford of the famous seventies show *Sanford and Son*, along with his pet tagline: "I'm just a tired old junkman, but ..." Another favorite was B. A. Baracus of the *A-Team*, always signing off with "I PITY THE FOOL!" Other frequent blog characters from TV Land included Road Runner, Stretch Cunningham from *All in the Family*, and Richie Cunningham from *Happy Days*.

After we exhausted one theme, we moved on to another. At some point nearly every member of the 1988 World Champion Los Angeles Dodgers appeared on the blog sites. I had no idea Orel Hershiser and the gang were with me—thanks, guys.

And then there was the German theme. When Chafee used the word "schadenfreude"[2] to describe his feelings of joy over his Democratic opponent's financial troubles, a new theme was born—blog in German. A blog alert, level 3, was quickly disseminated: "If you noticed this morning in the Projo, Chafee used a German word 'schadenfreude' to describe his feeling of satisfaction at Brown's problems. I have been instructed to ask all of you to please consider using a German word in your comments to annoy Chafee people." Fortunately, we actually had a close Laffey supporter who had studied German in college. The rest of the gang made good use of LEO (http://dict.leo.org), a Web site that provides English-to-German translations.

The same day the *Providence Journal* article appeared, the Laffey clan hit the blogs. Under a posting about school choice (www.anchorrising.com), the following pro-Laffey comments appeared with a delightful sprinkling of German dialect:

Just a few comments:

Eins - *Laffey is way out in front of the school choice issue. This is indeed the type of leadership that will draw a majority of Rhode Islanders to vote for him over Herr Chafee.*

Zwei - *Herr Chafee is nowhere to be found on the school choice issue. Like John Conyers and the Clintons, he supports school choice for his children but not others. How charakterlos.*[3]

Posted by oz at March 5, 2006 6:59 PM

Grundsatzdebatten im Augenblick!
  Piep piep![4]

Posted by roadrunner at March 5, 2006 8:14 PM

German is such an economical language. The following two words (der Idiot) encompass all these English translations: Fool, imbecile, moron, blockhead, dingbat, dufus, dork, ninny, and numskull. However, if one wants to use a modifier with idiot, such as "blithering" idiot or "complete" idiot, then der Vollidiot would be in order.

Lackey translates as "der Lakai."
Horseshoe as "das Hufeisen."

I think we have covered the essential argot pertaining to the Chafee campaign. There will be no further lessons necessary.

Posted by bountyhunter at March 5, 2006 11:30 PM

Another blog-related incident many on the campaign recall fondly is one we refer to as "hard cider," hence the title of this section. It all began with an innocent press release—well, maybe not that innocent—put out by Solly on February 22, 2006, entitled "Senator Chafee Sends Lackey to Face Laffey." This release was in response to an ambush attempt by Chafee's campaign manager, Ian Lang. The previous day, I had gone on a local radio show with host TV *Survivor* star Helen Glover to discuss my recently unveiled prescription drug policy. Chafee, of course, was invited to come on the show, but instead of having the guts to call in like a regular candidate, he sent Lang to call in unannounced. Needless to say, my use of the word "lackey" did not endear me to Ian Lang, as I was to discover two days later at the *Providence Journal* Follies.

Every year, the Providence Journal Guild Union puts on a comedy show called the Newspaper Guild Ocean State Follies. It is the ultimate insider event, attended by politicians, reporters, and their entourages. I had just entered the ballroom at the Venus De Milo in Swansea, Massachusetts, just over the Rhode Island line, when I spied Ian Lang approaching me from across the room, appearing quite agitated and a little glassy-eyed.

"Lackey!" he yelled. "Who you calling a lackey?"

His nose got within a foot of mine, and being a teetotaler myself, I thought I discerned the distinct smell of alcohol. It was only seven o'clock, and I fervently hoped the Chafee campaign had sent along a designated driver.

Of course, I greeted Ian with a smile as if I had no idea what he was talking about and said, "Ian, how are you? Hope you're doing okay!" Jordo—all six feet four of him—and others moved in, and Ian quickly backed off in the general direction of the bar area.

Somehow, this incident hit the blogosphere quickly. Within forty-eight hours, Bountyhunter, the most intellectual and one of the most dedicated of the blogging clan, alerted the blog world to the cross-border (the Rhode Island border, that is) incident in a comment under an unrelated post (www.anchorrising.com) about the United Arab Emirates port deal:

Talking about fighting - While Laffey fights for the taxpayers and for the safety of the populace, the Chafee people are apparently fighting for their own respect and sobriety.

Did anyone else hear or see that smackdown on Friday between Ian Lang and Steve Laffey? Get this - Lang actually called Laffey out, got in his face, and probably committed misdemeanor assault on the

Mayor. Apparently the hard cider at the Follies got to him and he felt compelled to defend his honor in some kind of new-age Aaron Burr style.

It looked as if Laffey handled the matter gracefully - dare I say senatorially - with a comment seemingly expressing compassion for the poor guy and a plea for him to sober up before driving home.

If I had to constantly defend Chafee's positions and be forced to debate Laffey on the radio, I would probably be hitting the hard cider myself - with vigor. Now we know why his boss refuses to debate Laffey.

Posted by bountyhunter at February 26, 2006 10:12 AM

Bountyhunter's incisive remarks were quickly followed up by the following keen observation on the part of Leon Berg:

Just wanted to point out that Chafee now has a national debt clock on his website. He's stealing Laffey's ideas!

Also, in the press release that the Chafee campaign put out criticizing Laffey for introducing school choice in Rhode Island, the word "unnecessary" was misspelled. Maybe Ian Lang wrote the press release after he got drunk at the Follies Friday night!

Posted by Leon Berg at March 1, 2006 11:39 AM

And the irrepressible Bountyhunter could not resist one more jab:

Lang the lackey must also have been drunk when he created "Linc's plan to balance the budget" for the website (directly underneath that annoying clock), which is also a response to Laffey's learned and detailed policy prescriptions. Here is the Chafee scheme - and brace yourselves for the intellectual rigor: "Don't spend it if you can't pay for it." That's it. That is the entire "plan." It is not a plan; it is a statement. At least he did not spell any of the words wrong. Perhaps that is because none of them are more than one syllable.

Posted by bountyhunter at March 1, 2006 12:08 PM

Whether or not the blog wars accomplished much of anything, we may never know. Who knows if we actually got under the Chafee camp's skin? (We did, however, hear rumors of disgruntlement.) Who knows whether the press checked out the blogs and actually waded through the broken German comments? But one thing I know for sure: the blog wars mattered to us. It kept the wider Laffey gang together and allowed supporters who didn't have a lot of time or a lot of money to contribute and play a role in the initial months of the campaign. But most of all, it was a great excuse to laugh, and it took some of the pressure off the natural stress of campaign life. In other countries, political disagreements don't end quite so amicably. From Peter the Great to Vladimir Putin, Russian leaders have a history of solving political conflicts with violence. Thank God for America, Al Gore, and the Internet.

THE BEST FRIENDS A GUY COULD ASK FOR

From the very beginning to the very end, I could count on a key group of supporters to do whatever was needed. Sometimes these tasks were enjoyable, but sometimes they were mind-numbingly dull. Out of all the things we asked volunteers to do, nothing was more painful than calling and identifying voters at our computerized call center three times a week. Chafee had the national

Republican Party and its famous Voter Vault working hard on his behalf (more on that in Chapter 9), but all I had was a mission and the best friends a guy could ask for.

If you live in a state with a competitive race, you probably received more than your fair share of these calls. It usually involves questions like "Can Mayor Laffey count on your support in the September 12 primary?" or "Do you consider yourself more pro-life or more pro-choice?" You keep asking yourself, *Aren't I on that no-call list?* but I'm afraid to tell you that the no-call list only applies to telemarketers, giving political pollsters free rein to interrupt your dinner and wake up your children. As the father of five children, I know it must be frustrating from your end. But let me assure you—in the spirit of misery loves company—it was just as painful from ours. And I speak from personal experience, because sometimes I would hold my fingers to my nose, disguise my voice, and make some of the calls myself. B-O-R-I-N-G.

The amazing thing is that the volunteers came back week after week, some as young as sixteen and some as old as seventy. Some of these folks I knew since I was a kid, like Eddie and Jackie, but others were new volunteers like Sean and John, who traveled at least thirty minutes each night to get from their Barrington homes to the call center in Cranston. These volunteers were like a grassroots army—much like in *Red Dawn*—ready to be deployed whenever needed. They got up at three in the morning on the Fourth of July to help gather the one thousand signatures I needed to get my name on the ballot, in accordance with Rhode Island state law. They participated in pre-debate rallies and out-yelled the Chafee folks. They wrote letters to the editor and dominated the blogosphere with panache. And throughout it all, they never lost their commitment or their sense of humor.

If there were two things that bound the Laffey camp together—and that the Chafee camp lacked—it was a fervent belief in the Republican cause we were fighting for and an inherent ability to laugh at ourselves as much as we laughed at everybody else. We dealt with serious issues on a daily basis, but we never fell into the trap of taking ourselves too seriously.

Politics is not for the soft of heart or for the thin-skinned. This was especially true in my case, running against one of the biggest special interests of all–the national Republican Party (the other being the national Democratic Party). Every day, I'd turn on my television, as would my supporters, and hear about some new horrible crime I had committed. Did you know Laffey doctored his résumé? Did you know that Laffey doesn't like senior citizens? For some, these kinds of insidious attacks could be demoralizing, as they were meant to be. Not to us. Much like my meeting with the NRSC back in the spring of 2005, these attacks were merely further vindication of our cause, and another reason to laugh.

Even a couple of months after I lost, supporters still came up to me and tell me that, win or lose, they would do it all over again. Same here. To be sure, the Laffey campaign worked its tail off, but we had a whale of a time doing it.

CHAPTER 8

Rules of the Road

Suddenly everyone is running. "Let's go man!" Hollers Eddie Curran, who grew up with Laffey in Cranston and serves as his main advance man. "Let's go! Let's go! Let's go!"–The Phoenix 9/6/06

When I decided to run for the U.S. Senate, I didn't want to give up on the time I spent with my family. A lot of candidates assume that it's simply part of the job description, but it was not a sacrifice I was willing to make. On the other hand, traveling across the state with five children packed in an SUV, four of them under eleven years old, wasn't feasible either. How many times can you listen to "Dad! Sam's leaning on me!" before you go out of your mind? When I ran for mayor of Cranston, it wasn't as much of a problem. Cranston may be Rhode Island's third largest city but it is still relatively small and easy enough for Kelly to swing by the house if the kids needed a nap or a diaper change. And though you can drive from one end of Rhode Island to the other in less than an hour, anyone with a wailing two-year-old knows that that's not close enough.

I had a genuine dilemma on my hands, but I have always believed that every problem has a solution waiting to be born. One night in January 2006, I lay in bed, my eyes wide open, when it hit me: A thirty-one-foot Class C recreational vehicle plastered with Laffey U.S. Senate signs. It would be the ultimate campaign vehicle, and it would keep the Laffey family together. Kelly and I devised a game plan. There would be no sports this year for the Laffey clan. No baseball, no soccer, no birthday parties. Just the seven of us, packed into our family RV, making one big Laffey push to win this race. Turns out, we didn't win the race, but buying the RV was one of the best family decisions we ever made.

When the last of New England's winter had faded, I purchased a beautiful RV, officially christened the Rhody Reformer, with plenty of beds, a television, an oven, a bathroom,[1] and even a shower, Though April was still a chilly thirty-five degrees in the morning, it was officially spring, and that was good enough for me. "Spring has sprung!" I told a local reporter at a campaign stop, as the rest of the group shivered underneath their scarves and gloves, giving me the evil eye when they thought I wasn't looking. We were ready to hit the road running.

"RUNNING AGAINST THE BIG SHOTS"

As reporters from all around the country flooded into Rhode Island to report on the race, the Laffey campaign became well-known for its evening and weekend blitzes. A blitz is an old-fashioned door-to-door grassroots ground game. If you're reading this in California or Texas or any state other than Little Rhody, you've probably never had a statewide candidate stop and ring your doorbell. But being the smallest state in the Union, Rhode Island is probably the only state where knocking on doors makes sense. In one night, we'd meet anywhere from one hundred to two hundred voters, and they'd all tell their friends that Steve Laffey knocked on their doors and shook their hands. In Rhode Island, where the largest Republican primary turnout to date was forty-five thousand people, two hundred voters a night could make a difference.

When Joe Klein of *Time* magazine and *Primary Colors* fame tagged along on a blitz in the western Rhode Island town of Coventry, he titled his article "Running Against the Big Shots," and he meant "run" in every sense of the word. There was no walking on the Laffey blitzes. I wore sneakers, going through several pairs over the years, and advised reporters tagging along to do the same. The smart ones listened, but invariably, there were one or two scrambling to keep up in their heels and designer loafers. Maybe heels were okay when you accompanied Chafee on one of his country club tours, but when you campaigned with the Laffey clan, it was all sweat all the time. As summer heated up, I often went through two or three yellow polo shirts in one night.

Every Saturday—and when the primary got closer, a couple of nights a week—my campaign staff and a host of friends and volunteers met at my house at the appointed time. On Saturday mornings, this meant eight o'clock, bleary eyes, and lots of coffee. **Rule #1:** *Don't knock on anyone's door on a Saturday morning before nine.* During the week, it meant four-thirty in the afternoon and push until dark. **Rule #2:** *No one wants to talk to you when they can't see your face.*

No blitz was complete without Kelly and the kids. With their matching blue and yellow outfits, they were an integral part of the Laffey team. Blue on safety yellow had been the Laffey colors since day one of my first mayoral campaign when Tom Marcelle informed me that I had only two color combinations to choose from. He had read a study claiming that when people are driving down the road, their eyes are attracted to two color schemes more than any other: black on orange and blue on safety yellow. Since Halloween only comes once a year, we discarded the black on orange combo and went with blue on safety yellow. From that moment, every item of clothing was purchased with the color scheme in mind, including blue and yellow Converse sneakers for the entire family, inscribed with "Laffey 2006" above the heel.

Off we went, eight of us packed into the Rhody Reformer, with six cars following behind. Harry the Greek was at the head of the line, driving the RV and screaming on the cell phone, "I'm putting that sign up tomorrow! You get those two short Chinese guys! You know, the grass is taller than their heads. You hear me . . . Just get the hell out of bed; I don't need no shit on this!" When reporters came along, Harry dutifully omitted the ethnic references. Ditto on the profanity.

Each week, my trusty campaign coordinator, Jordo, chose Republican-leaning neighborhoods based on prior voting records. We headed to Cumberland, to Woonsocket, to North Kingstown—anywhere there were people living in close proximity. Thus, **Rule #3:** *When knocking on doors, make sure you can get from one house to the next without gasping for breath.*

Once we reached our destination, George's F-350 led the way, crawling down the street with speakers packed in the back, blasting patriotic music interspersed with announcements of my arrival. "Come see Senate candidate Steve Laffey, the only Senate candidate on Sun Valley Drive," George proclaimed. "Shake hands with the man who saved the City of Cranston! Steve Laffey is the only candidate who will fight the special interests in Washington!"

I stood in the middle of the street, waiting for the call that always triggered a running start. Door knockers dispersed to the left and to the right, while one lead volunteer with voter registration lists in hand directed them to registered Independent and Republican households. Someone hollered "Mayor!" and I was off, running to meet Mrs. Jones or Mr. Smith, or whoever wanted to speak with me.

CONVERSATIONS

One of the many great things about the campaign was the opportunity to meet people from all over the state. From Woonsocket to Westerly, from North Providence to Newport, from Scituate to South Kingstown, I had the opportunity to see up close what makes America tick. Who are the men and women who are the backbone of this great country? After a year of knocking on thousands of doors and clocking thousands of miles throughout Rhode Island, I can tell you that they are often people who like to wear as little clothing as possible when they open the door.

If you turned on the mainstream news or opened up the *New York Times*, you might think voters in Rhode Island only wanted to talk about the war in Iraq, President Bush, or abortion. When national reporters came up to cover the race, they all wanted to know the same thing: how does a real Republican who is pro-life and against gay marriage win in Rhode Island? To be sure, these are important issues, but I've knocked on thousands of doors over the past year, and I almost never got a question about abortion or gay marriage. Regular folks living in vinyl-sided houses and mowing their own lawns were mostly concerned with the issues that impacted their daily lives. Property taxes, education, corruption—this is what people wanted to talk about. And on one particular Sunday morning, in the beautiful coastal city of Middletown, Rhode Island, nearly every person—Republican, Democrat, and Independent—wanted to talk about crabgrass.

I approached the first house where a middle-aged man stood on a ladder painting his second-floor shutters. I approached carefully. The last thing you want to hear on a campaign is "Whoa!" and then a crash.

"Excuse me, sir." His head turned to face me. "I don't mean to interrupt you, and please don't—don't fall off that ladder, but I'm

Steve Laffey, and I'm running for the U.S. Senate. I'd like your vote, and I'd be happy to answer any questions you might have."

"Yeah, I got a question. What's going on with the crabgrass?"

"Crabgrass?" I echoed.

"Yeah, crabgrass . . . Out in front, it's taking over my lawn. The city planted it, and now I don't know what to do with it."

Now, I wanted the guy's vote, but I thought, *I'm running for the U.S. Senate—I can't do anything about the crabgrass! My front lawn is full of crabgrass and I couldn't give a hoot.* Of course, I didn't actually say any of that. Instead, I was polite as could be and said, "Well, sir, I'm running for the U.S. Senate, and I can't do much about this local problem. But I'll tell you this, right now, I'm the mayor of Cranston, and I would never allow crabgrass up there. Let me just leave this brochure with you and you can take a look at it later."

"Sure, no problem. Hey, aren't you the guy that got rid of those crossing guards?"

"Yes, sir, that was me."

"That was damn good." From the distance, I heard the one word I longed to hear at times like this: "Mayor!" And I was off.

Over the next couple of houses, I received a crash course in Middletown's municipal grass program. I quickly discovered that the city of Middletown controlled the first couple of feet of land off the street, and instead of laying down sidewalk, the city planted grass. Apparently, the quality of this grass left something to be desired.

Instead of talking about cutting taxes or stopping Alaska's Bridge to Nowhere, I got an earful on crabgrass. Tip O'Neill was right: all politics is local. So I adapted. After ten houses and six conversations about crabgrass, I became an expert. Starting with the eleventh house, I introduced myself and said, "I'm very concerned about this crabgrass problem. What the heck is going on here? As the mayor of Cranston, I would never stand for that in my city!"

When in Rome . . .

Everywhere we went, people wanted to talk about something different. The thing you learn on the campaign trail is that every person has his own story to tell, with his own problems and his own hopes and dreams. For every one of Rhode Island's thirty-nine cities and towns, I met Rhode Islanders who struggled just to get by. As I listened to their moving stories, I couldn't help but wonder about all the nonsense that came along with political campaigns—the outlandish TV commercials and the underhanded shenanigans—that had nothing to do with the real people I met daily and their problems.

There was a single mom with two children living in Westerly whom I hadn't seen since my senior year in high school. She told me that her ex-husband used to beat her, and she suffered debilitating strokes because of him. Another lady in Coventry introduced me to her epileptic daughter and asked how she was supposed to afford the medication her daughter needed. And sometimes the people I met weren't even eligible to vote, like children on street corners selling lemonade. They had their own stories, too.

I have five kids, so I understand lemonade stands. It is the ultimate American experience: the young entrepreneur, usually eight or nine, trying to make a buck off a product that isn't particularly sellable. Unlike Chafee, who claimed during one of our debates that "the reason America's at the top of the world is our great social programs," I subscribe to a different theory. I believe lemonade stands make America great. And no matter where we were or what we were doing, if I saw a lemonade stand, I made Harry pull over and treated the whole gang to a little slice of Americana.

"Hey, guys," I'd say to the young entrepreneurs. "What are you selling today?"

"Lemonade and cookies. Would you like some?"

"Would I like some? Of course, we want lots of lemonade and throw in some of those cookies. How much are you charging?"

"Fifteen cents."

"Fifteen cents? You guys need to raise your prices. There is a very inelastic demand for lemonade on a hot summer day." The words "inelastic demand" always brought giggles from the kids. But I swear, they appreciated this economics lesson more than some folks down in Washington, especially those who think a windfall profits tax on oil companies is a good idea.

To me, there is nothing more American than watching nine-year-olds grab plastic cups with their grubby hands, picking their noses, and handing me several cups of diluted Country Time lemonade, usually warm. Buying lemonade—actually drinking it was something I left to my compadres on the RV—was my way of connecting with the future of this country. As long as we have children selling lemonade on street corners, I know we'll be okay.

Some people wanted to talk about my dad's struggle with Alzheimer's. Some of them actually knew my dad personally—this was Rhode Island after all. Some people wanted to talk about the proposed Narragansett Indian casino. And then there were the roofers in Smithfield. They wanted to talk—actually yell—about illegal immigration.

It was the weekend before the Fourth of July. Just a couple of weeks after John McCain and Ted Kennedy pushed their amnesty bill through the Senate, the debate over illegal immigration had reached a fever pitch. As I blitzed through the town of Smithfield, my second yellow polo shirt nearly soaked through, I heard a sudden cry from the rooftops.

"Hey, Mr. Laffey!" I turned around, searching out the sound of the booming voice. "Over here, Mr. Laffey!" I looked up, my hand perched on my forehead to shield my eyes from the glare of the late-morning sun. A group of tough-talking roofers stood atop the house in front of me, their tools in hand, some with shirts, more without, and all sweating something terrible.

"I like what you did in Cranston!" the leader of the group bellowed. "But what the hell are you going to do about illegal immigration? These guys"—he pointed around to the others—"are all losing work to illegal immigrants. You've got people hiring these illegals, doing shoddy work, paying them half what these guys make, and hurting my business."

"Secure the borders first!" I yelled back. "Those Washington clowns just don't get it! They're putting up a smokescreen and hope you don't notice. If we can put a man on the moon, we can put up a fence to protect our country. And after we do that, we start throwing some employers in jail! Then everyone will get the message! You know my opponent supports amnesty. I won't stand for it. Help me get down to Washington and get this done for you."

"Okay, Mayor Laffey! You got my vote!" they cried enthusiastically. And we were off, to the next door, to the next roof, to the next person who had his own story to tell. I was ready to listen.

At the time, I thought, *Wouldn't it be great, if and when Chafee actually agrees to debate, if the roofers asked the questions instead of the reporters.* The roofers wouldn't let Chafee get away with some half-baked answer like the one he offered on C-SPAN: "When people talk about securing the borders I have the memory of the vast, vast open country, how difficult it's going to be, and also, what would make these people go through that kind of country, rattlesnakes, no water, and miles and miles of emptiness . . . that's our challenge." *Wouldn't it be great if the woman in Westerly got to ask Chafee herself why he never came knocking on her door, or if middle-class folks had a chance to ask him why he voted to raise their taxes by $1,800?*[2] They wouldn't let Chafee hem and haw about snakes and the Concord Coalition. No one cares about snakes and talking points. They just want their problems solved.

THE BLITZ GOES NATIONAL–THANKS, JOE!

Reporters loved blitzing with us, and we loved having them. In fact, our favorite Washington-based reporter became an honorary member of the team, joining us on blitz after blitz, fed up with chasing the Chafee campaign down. But it wasn't until Joe Klein's "Running Against the Big Shots" article in *Time* that the Laffey blitz–described by Klein as a "mystical average-folks communion"– caught the attention of the national media.

After that, everyone wanted a piece of the blitz: from the *Houston Chronicle* to the *New York Times*, from Fox News Channel to the *Daily Telegraph* in London, from BBC to Japanese television. A normal blitz would have four or five reporters walking along with me, several gasping to keep up, and one or two camera crews with their boom mikes over my head. The trick was making sure Eddie knew I was miked so he wouldn't yell out, "Hey, Mayor, skip the blue house! The lady over there's cousin was a Cranston crossing guard. She pretty much hates you."

The children ate up the media attention and often featured in it. My nine-year-old daughter, Sarah, headlined a front-page *Boston Globe* story about the race. In an article titled "Brash GOP Challenger Presses Chafee in R.I.," journalist Rick Klein reported:

> *The Laffey campaign's secret weapon wears sneakers with tiny wheels on the bottom. She's Stephen Laffey's 9-year-old daughter, and at Cranston's annual Greek Festival on Saturday, she made her famously brash father look shy, cutting sharp paths through the festival grounds to offer handshakes to anyone who would take them. "I'm Sarah Laffey," she said. "My dad's running for the US Senate."*

Over the year, I watched my kids grow up on the campaign trail. I remember walking down the street with reporters one hot summer day when I heard the familiar cry of "Mayor!"—only this time the voice belonged to my ten-year-old son, Sam. When I reached the door, I found Sam holding the door open, smiling broadly, no doubt proud of his self-imposed promotion from regular kid to campaign volunteer. He handed me a palm card and said flawlessly, "Mrs. Smith would be happy to talk with you, Mayor Laffey." I grabbed the card and spoke to Mrs. Smith, but I barely heard what she had to say as I fought back tears of pride.

The night of the second radio debate, I listened to Sam and Sarah pontificate about the race on air in a pre-debate show, marveling at the people they had become. How many nine-year-olds can make intelligent arguments on public radio? How many ten-year-olds walk up to a sitting U.S. senator and the man his father is running against to shake the senator's hand and ask him about his horses? Even Audrey, all of two years old then, loved climbing out of her stroller as we blitzed to shake voters' hands. "Wanna shake 'ands," she'd cry.

Running for the U.S. Senate was truly a family affair. It was a decision we made together, and it was a process we pursued until the very last day together, each of us knowing the rewards and the risks we might face along the way. *Win or lose,* I remember thinking on that summer day, the image of Sam standing tall, his smile wide, handing me a Laffey palm card, fresh in my mind, *it's worth it all.*

BEYOND BLITZING

On rainy days, all blitzes were off, a function of **Rule #4:** *Don't knock on doors in the pouring rain.* There is a thin line between aggressive and crazy, and it was a line we didn't want to cross. Instead, Harry drove the Rhody Reformer with a small entourage up a rural route as far away from Cranston as possible, and three or four of us worked our way back, stopping off at every small business, restaurant, and coffee shop along the way, sitting at people's tables, greeting voters, listening to their stories, and literally breaking bread.

When it came to rainy-day campaign stops, I was the king of **Rule #5:** *Order something in every store so the owners don't mind you greeting the customers.* The problem with this rule is that there's a lot of good food in Rhode Island. By noon, I had eaten the equivalent of several full meals. Granted, there are grazing diets, but something tells me those diets don't call for johnnycakes with syrup, two ham and cheese sandwiches, corn beef hash, a piece of apple pie, and half a Belgian waffle in the span of a couple of hours. I started the campaign at 174 pounds and ended it at 174 pounds, but I can't explain it. Maybe it was all that running.

Non-blitz nights were filled with community events: outdoor music festivals, steak fries, art shows, local fairs, parades, ethnic festivals, and everything in between. The goal was simple: meet every voter in Rhode Island. When I bumped into a familiar-looking fellow who exclaimed, "Hey, I met you at the art fair last week," I knew I was doing something right.

A typical summer night found the Laffey family and a bunch of volunteers heading off to National Night Out at Oakland Beach in Warwick and sweating in the hundred-degree weather. When it came to local events like the Oakland Beach festival, **Rule #6** was probably the most important: *Always park the RV with plenty of space around it.* The strategy behind this rule was twofold. One, it was crucial that all voters be able to see the massive Elect Laffey signs plastered on the RV. Two, it was critical that we be able to get out when we needed to. This process often involved Harry resorting to all sorts of dubious tactics, but Harry never disappointed. Harry could park the RV in a phone booth if I asked him to.

Left to his own devices, Harry concocted a host of reasons why no one could park within a twenty-foot radius of the Rhody Reformer. Sometimes, he told people he was saving the spot for the governor, whether the governor was coming or not. Sometimes he claimed he was reserving the space for the state troopers, as if the state troopers need Harry to save them a parking spot. On this particular night, he let people know, out of the goodness of his Greek heart, that "someone got a flat tire. There's probably nails in the dirt—I'm lookin' for 'em right now. You go park over there." Whatever the reason, Harry made sure no one blocked our portable Elect Laffey signage. And no one ever did.

With the RV safe in Harry's hands, I greeted folks and introduced them to the kids, devouring a Philly cheese steak and a host of free food along the way. I had already sweated through one shirt when I saw the Free Massage sign and headed over to engage the owner, a grape Fanta in hand. In accordance with **Rule #7—** *Take advantage of everything free*—I couldn't resist the massage even though my campaign manager, John Dodenhoff, attempted to dissuade me. "Mayor, aren't you a little sweaty for that?"

"Oh no, I'm just fine, thanks, John."

For the next five minutes, I lay facedown, enjoying my free massage while I pontificated with a group of people I couldn't see about the need for a simpler and fairer tax plan.

Following the massage, we headed closer to the water, spotting the Keep Chafee booth, sans Chafee, and an inviting pile of pizza boxes across the walkway, all taped up with no ownership. First things first. I walked right up to the Chafee group, offered them my brightest smile, shook their hands, slapped them on the back, and wished them well.

"Hey, you guys look good, love the signs, everything all right? How're you doing . . . Is the senator here? . . . Oh, he's not? . . . Oh, well. I'm here . . . Maybe next time."

Moving on, I headed for the pizza, noticing the Caserta logo on the boxes. Note: Caserta is the gold standard of pizza in Rhode Island.[3] Assuming the pizza was free, like the rest of the food I'd just devoured, I eagerly opened a box and helped myself to some pepperoni and cheese.

It didn't take long for others to notice and line up. Who doesn't want free Caserta pizza? As I handed out pizza slices to the hungry throng, it occurred to me that it appeared as if the Laffey campaign had sponsored the pizza table. In accordance with **Rule #8**—*There are always votes in serving people food*—I did nothing to dissuade them.

Thirty to forty people had gathered round, enjoying the upscale delights of Caserta's pizza and complimenting me on the provisions, when I noticed the Chafee crowd growing agitated and, out of my left peripheral vision, a short gray-haired lady approaching fast—too fast to be a pizza-loving Laffey fan—so I lowered my pizza and moved off. By now, there were only a couple of slices left, no doubt the reason behind her rant. "What's going on here?" I heard her cry as I slunk away. "No one was supposed to open this until seven o'clock! This pizza was supposed to help . . ."

"It was Laffey!" the Chafee group chanted. "It was Laffey!"

I'm still waiting for the formal FEC complaint and the front-page *Providence Journal* headline: "Laffey Makes Off with Caserta Pizza, Offers No Defense."

From the pizza, I headed over to the navy recruiters booth, where they were giving away a poster if you could do forty-five military push-ups without stopping. Well, I couldn't let a couple of slices of pizza, a large Philly cheese steak, and a grape soda slow me down. So down I went and did forty-five push-ups, one more than my age, thanking the Lord it was only forty-five and not fifty. The poster was mine.

Finally, it was time to leave. By the end of the night, I tallied two polo shirts soaked through with sweat, too much food to list, five hundred potential voters, one free poster, and an angry group of Chafee workers. By all counts, it was a great night. And tomorrow, we would do it all over again.

The next morning I was up at five, ready to go. Unlike Chafee, who once told the Associated Press that "he'd rather be home watching a golf tournament" than shaking hands with voters outside a supermarket, I loved every second of campaigning. I love meeting people, and I love the energy.

My motto on the campaign was go wherever the voters go. Unfortunately for my volunteers, this meant hauling them out of bed at five in the morning and standing in traffic holding Laffey signs and waving to commuters on their way to work. Reporters asked me why I bothered, and I explained that fighting for Rhode Island taxpayers is a full-time job. If I was willing to stand in thirty-five-degree weather holding an I'm Laffey sign as cars whipped by, then people would understand just how hard I was willing to work on their behalf. "You know what they know?" I told an AP reporter. "It's six-thirty in the morning, and I'm out working." Many reporters didn't get it, but the folks on the road sure did. Supporters honked, offered their thumbs up, a V for victory, or simply rolled down their windows and yelled, "I hope you win!" Some Laffey lovers were so enthusiastic that they waved as they zipped by, a cigarette in one hand, a coffee in the other (one lady even had a dog on her lap to go with the cigarette and coffee), and three fingers grasping at the steering wheel. I appreciated their dedication but would have forgone the wave for the sake of public safety.

Don't get me wrong—for every dozen people beeping their horns, there were a couple who gave the thumbs down or the more eloquent middle finger up. We smiled and shouted, "Thank you! Thank you, sir!" You could see their confusion on their rearview mirrors, but by then it was too late. They were beyond us.

When dealing with the enemy, there is only one way to win: smother them with love.

These Laffey haters couldn't stand the idea that it was six o'clock in the morning and I was already out there working my tail off. No doubt, a commuter picked up his cell phone, called the Chafee camp, and left a message: "I'm in front of Apple Valley Mall, and Laffey's there holding signs. Where are you?" They may have disliked me for a whole number of reasons—some legitimate—but what they hated most was that nothing they did mattered. No matter how many negative ads the Chafee camp and NRSC ran, no matter how many angry fingers they gave us, no matter what they yelled from their windows, I was going to fight for the taxpayers until the very end.

And fight we did. From morning to night, we went to every event we could find. Some we were invited to, and some . . . "Surprise, surprise! Funny to see you all here." This included pretty much every ethnic event in the state of Rhode Island, from the Jewish Purim parade (my favorite—gotta love those hamantaschen)[4] to the Jamaican festival where Sarah and I danced to Bob Marley's "Jamming," to a Providence festival commemorating India's sixtieth Independence Day.

The best part about these campaign stops was that I met people I never expected to meet. When I arrived at the India Independence Day festival, I sat down next to an elderly gentleman sitting by himself, only to discover that this gentleman was actually a much decorated Indian general who had served under the American general Douglas MacArthur in World War II. General Eustace D'Souza had traveled thousands of miles just to give the keynote speech at the Providence event.

Boy was I surprised when General D'Souza got up to speak and announced to the hundred-plus crowd: "That young man over there, Mayor Laffey, needs to be in the United States Senate. We have to help him get elected." I nearly fell off my chair when he ended his speech with the same rousing endorsement: "Mayor Laffey, the mayor of the next city over"—he even pointed in the right direction—"has to get to the United States Senate. I hope you will all vote for him."

LESSONS FROM THE ROAD

Liddy Dole and the national Republican establishment in Washington were against me, but I had General D'Souza and the morning commuters, with a few exceptions. I had the restaurant owners, the Smithfield roofers, the disgruntled residents of Middletown, the Caserta pizza lovers, the Reagan Democrats who wanted change—and the Glen Myerses of the world. Glen told me as I knocked on his door in Coventry, "I believe in you. And I hope you beat the pants off of Lincoln Chafee."

If I learned one thing from the time I spent campaigning across Rhode Island, it is that Reagan's commonsense ideals are very much alive and well in the hearts of men and women in this country—and in the case of General D'Souza, India, too! I often wondered during the campaign if our country would be run differently if Liddy Dole and the other Washington insiders had to knock on doors, stand on street corners, and answer real people's questions. How would they act if they saw people as they really lived, many paycheck to paycheck? What would they answer to the roofers in Smithfield who wanted to know why their jobs were going to illegal aliens? What would they tell party devotees who wanted to know why the size of government had increased so much under a Republican president and a Republican Congress? And what would they answer when local Republicans wanted to know how the party could support a person who didn't stand up for Republicans?

I can just imagine Liddy Dole in her perfectly pressed suit standing at a doorway in Hopkington, trying to explain to a middle-aged restaurant owner, his belly hanging dangerously over his waistline, that "Lincoln Chafee is the only person who can keep the seat in Rhode Island." The fellow would listen to Dole's perfectly attuned talking points, and then he'd abruptly end the conversation, yelling, "Linc Chafee is no Republican!"

And what would Liddy Dole say then? We're still waiting for an answer.

CHAPTER 9

The Final Days:
Desperation and the Invasion of Outsiders

"I find it interesting that Senator Chafee has the gall to ask Democrats to do something he just can't bring himself to do: Change party affiliation. Seems pretty hypocritical."–Bren, blog post, Anchor Rising, April 21, 2006

Outlandish personal attacks on the campaign trail are usually the hallmarks of desperation. If a candidate is leading by ten points, he doesn't run commercials attacking his opponent's hat size. But when a candidate is behind, clinging to his political career by a thread, the aim of the game is to throw as much mud as he can dig up and hope more falls on his opponent than on himself.

The public saw examples of these kinds of desperate last-minute attacks all around the country. Rhode Island was no different, except for the fact that the NRSC directed its guerrilla warfare at a fellow Republican and saw no reason to wait until the last minute. These tactics started early in the campaign, with the NRSC's first ad attacking me for helping oil companies make money, and carried on to the very last moment, when the NRSC accused me of disenfranchising voters in Cranston.

The problem with desperation is that it feeds on itself like a cancer. Left untreated, it divides and grows, and tactics that seemed unacceptable in May and June become necessary in August and September. This was to be expected, given Chafee's own admission to the *Washington Post* just days before the primary that he had "deep apprehensions" about his ability to win. If Chafee and the NRSC were desperate in May and June, they had reached full-fledged panic mode by September. Unfortunately, panic makes people do some awfully silly things.

JACKVONY REDUX AND OTHER INANITIES

It wasn't all that surprising when Chafee's last-minute attempt to derail my candidacy featured Randy Jackvony of pixelation fame. When political chicanery surfaced, the distinct handiwork of Randy Jackvony was usually not too far behind. Like the Energizer Bunny, Jackvony kept going and going and going . . .

On September 6, a mere six days before the primary, my press secretary, Solly, received an e-mail containing a voice attachment from a local reporter. When she double-clicked on the attachment, she heard the following voice-mail message and the distinct sound of my voice:

> *Randy, it's Laffey. I'm really pissed off. I'm calling you directly. I don't need fuckin' comments like that in the paper. At all. I never need them. On small issues like this. I need your fuckin' help. I'm at—uh, you probably can't even reach me. 802-533-2519. [Click.]*

The most important thing you need to know about this voice mail is that it was *three years old*. I kid you not. Three years before, when Randy Jackvony was still a Cranston city councilman, I left this message for him in a calm but stern voice while I was up in Vermont, wondering why he was siding with the Democrats in a minor political dispute without so much as a phone call. Apparently, Jackvony was not very pleased with my message and decided to save it, in digital format no less. Three years later, Jackvony and the Chafee campaign hand-delivered the voice mail to *Providence*

Journal reporters as last-minute proof of "a mean-spirited man who trounces upon those who don't see things his way." I guess they were talking about me.

My Washington consultant advised me to apologize. I told him thanks but no thanks, and had Solly release the following statement: "Regarding Randy Jackvony, while only he can understand why he kept a voice mail for three years, we hope he's doing well." At least I was being kind. One local talk radio host called Jackvony a "pantywaist."

I have no problem apologizing when the situation calls for it, but I wasn't going to pretend to be something I wasn't. Yeah, I swear sometimes. Granted, it's not the greatest habit, but neither is using my car as a trash receptacle for my many half-eaten muffins. For the majority of folks who grew up like I did, a voice mail would not prove me to be mean and scary, but rather to be a person who was just like them. In fact, the day the article ran in the *Providence Journal*, I walked out of Cranston City Hall, greeted by two city workers, who between laughs called out, "Jeez, Mayor—you swear? Never would have guessed it!"

This desperate attack by the Chafee camp proved to be the single funniest moment of the entire campaign. To this day, many of my friends have set their ringers to play this message when I call. And I still chuckle every time I hear it.

On a serious note, though, "gotcha" politics like this is one of the reasons why people don't run for public office and why people don't vote. They want to know how their money is being spent or how we're going to secure the borders, but they tune out when they hear "Steve Laffey swears!" or "Steve Laffey has an ego the size of Texas!" This kind of silliness doesn't affect their lives. As Solly told reporters that day, "Senator Chafee is disgracing the office of the United States Senate by spending the last five days of his campaign digging through private conversations and throwing mud instead of talking about the real issues and real problems that people struggle with. Mayor Laffey only feels pity for him. We all await the next ridiculous attack."

We didn't have to wait long. Liddy Dole jumped on the bandwagon, targeting primary voters with her own personal taped phone message, accusing me of having a "history of troubling and inflammatory behavior." When I heard this, I tried to imagine Ronald Reagan leaving this kind of message, but I couldn't. President Reagan simply had too much integrity.

The day before Jackvony approached the *Providence Journal*, a mysterious group calling themselves Republicans Who Care (in contrast to all the Republicans who don't care?) bought $100,000 worth of negative ads, claiming that "my last two jobs as a stockbroker ended in disgrace." Turns out, Republicans Who Care is a front for the "Let's raise everyone's taxes and call it fiscal responsibility" Republican Main Street Partnership, a group of "moderate" Republicans, including Christine Todd Whitman and David Rockefeller. Apparently, they think it's their party, too.

Whether it was digging up three-year-old voice mails, lying outright, or sending college kids to drive by my house with a video camera to spy on me and my family—something my wife did not appreciate very much—the Chafee camp and its surrogates never seemed too troubled by their own integrity problems, just the ones they claimed I had. Without any substantive ideas to put forward, the Chafee camp campaigned on fear, and as their own fear became more intense, so did the nature of their desperation and their attacks.

At the 2000 Republican National Convention in Philadelphia, vice-presidential nominee Dick Cheney articulated the difference between the two parties: "They [the Democrats] will make accusations. We will make proposals. They will feed fear. We will appeal to hope. They will offer more lectures, and legalisms, and carefully worded denials. We offer another way, a better way, and a stiff dose of truth." Six years later, as I listened to an NRSC lawyer accuse me of trying to steal the election, Dick Cheney's words rang painfully hollow.

THE INVASION OF OUTSIDERS

To its credit, the NRSC was not completely clueless. Liddy Dole knew that stupid attacks wouldn't win the primary. Not even last-minute evidence of profanity would do the trick. She also knew that if the Rhode Island race came down to Republican voters alone, Chafee was a goner, big-time. Republicans tolerated Chafee because he was "the best they could do," but given a choice between Linc Chafee and, well, anything short of a doorknob, there was no question where the numbers would fall. But the NRSC only had two options to choose from: Destroy my character or hijack the Republican primary. In the end, Liddy Dole liked both options so much she saw no reason to choose between them.

A little background: Rhode Island primaries are semi-open. Independent, or unaffiliated, voters—making up over 50 percent of Rhode Island's registered voter pool—can choose to vote in either the Republican or the Democratic primary. With no major state-wide primary on the Democratic side,[1] the NRSC, RNC, and Chafee campaign pinned all their hopes on getting enough liberals out to vote for Chafee. This was not a secret strategy. All three camps were more than open about their plan to throw Rhode Island Republicans under the proverbial bus. NRSC communications director Brian Nick admitted as much at a panel sponsored by the *National Journal*'s daily political blog, The Hotline (http://hotlineblog.nationaljournal.com), in December 2005. The following conversation occurred between Brian Nick and Guy Cecil, the Democratic Senatorial Campaign Committee's political director:

REPUBLICAN NICK: *Senator Chafee doesn't need Republicans to vote for him.*

DEMOCRATIC CECIL: *Well, he'll need a few Republicans to get through the primary, won't he?*

REPUBLICAN NICK: *No.*

In 2002 and 2004, Karl Rove and the Republican National Committee became famous for the GOP's vaunted get-out-the-vote effort. In previous years this effort had been used to find conservative-leaning voters. This was done through a process called microtargeting, a system that divides the voter market into small segments that can then be targeted with specific messages. For example, if you belonged to a local gun club or if you subscribed to *Investors Business Daily*, you might receive phone calls about a Republican candidate's pro-gun or pro-tax-cut positions. On the other hand, if you subscribed to *High Times* or belonged to the Sierra Club, Karl Rove probably crossed your name off his list. In Rhode Island, however, where the ironies were already too great to list, the celebrated get-out-the-vote effort was directed at liberals. In this case, if you were an avid reader of the *Nation* or if you sent an annual check to the American Civil Liberties Union, Karl Rove actually wanted you to come out and vote in the Rhode Island Republican primary for Linc Chafee. This reminded me of one of those old questions from the California Achievement Tests we took in grade school.

Which item doesn't belong?
A) Karl Rove
B) The Nation

C) *The ACLU*
D) *Linc Chafee*

I'm gonna go out on a limb and say ... A. Yeah, A. That's the ticket.

Like the desperate attacks on my character, the get-out-the-liberal-vote effort began early. According to the *Washington Post*, the strategy sessions were set into motion six months before primary when the NRSC "sat down with the Chafee campaign to construct a voter-turnout program. Weekly phone calls followed and a number of NRSC senior staffers—including political director Blaise Hazelwood—made regular trips to the state to ensure the structure was being built."

The first part of this plan was getting Democrats to disaffiliate and register as Independents before Rhode Island's June 14 disaffiliation deadline passed. Chafee's wife, Stephanie née Danforth, sent out e-mails urging Democrats to disaffiliate for the day, explaining that "immediately after voting, you can get a disaffiliation form from the clerk at the polling station and change your registration back to your initial party affiliation." Rhode Island Republicans, ticked off by the hijacking of their primary, aptly referred to this effort as "rent a Democrat for a day."

Once the disaffiliation deadline passed, the NRSC targeted Independent voters, urging them to come out on Election Day and vote for Chafee. This process, though, required bodies, and unlike my campaign, which was made up of grassroots volunteers from Rhode Island, Senator Chafee had a little trouble in the recruitment department. Never fear, the Republican National Committee swooped into the state, pumping over $400,000 into a massive voter-mobilization drive, importing an army of out-of-state workers and paid staff to Rhode Island to knock on doors, make phone calls, and do whatever was needed to get out the liberal vote.

Not to be left out, Brock Bierman, last seen in Chapter 1 fleeing the room, coordinated with a Virginia-based group called Republican Rapid Responders to bring in an additional legion of out-of-state "volunteers." In early August, the following e-mail was sent to Republicans around the country:

> Dear Rapid Responders,
>
> On September 12, 2006 one of the most important primary elections for the Republican Party will take place in the State of Rhode Island.
>
> The Republican National Committee has personally asked the RRRs to help recruit volunteers for deployment to Rhode Island for up to two weeks and as few as five days before the September 12th primary election . . . President Bush, Elizabeth Dole and Ken Mehlman have pledged their support to Senator Lincoln Chafee because they know we need to continue a strong majority in the US SENATE . . .
>
> **PLEASE NOTE: All expenses including airfare, lodging, and food will be provided for all volunteers.**

There you have it. The national Republicans' grand strategy for getting Linc Chafee reelected and holding on to the majority in the Senate: attack me personally, import out-of-state volunteers, and get liberals out to vote. In the end, our grassroots effort came close but could not overcome the enormous resources of the national Republican Party. We were out-spent two-to-one, and while we had great volunteers—the best you could find in Rhode Island—and a get-out-the-vote effort that began in January 2006, it fell short of competing with the vaunted get-out-the-vote effort of the national Republican Party.

Even the liberal blog Daily Kos (www.dailykos.com) noted the extremes to which the national Republican Party went to drag Chafee across the finish line. In a November 30 post, blogger Markos Moulitsas Zúniga offered his post-election analysis:

It wasn't just the millions that Liddy Dole dumped into Chafee's campaign . . . For three weeks, the NRSC took its troops out of Maryland, New Jersey, Ohio, Virginia, Pennsylvania, Tennessee, and Missouri to rescue Chafee's ass in a primary, even though he was always a long-shot to retain the seat.

What Zúniga saw clearly was that time, money, and people matter. A happy man, he ends with this parting shot: "Liddy Dole for NRSC chair in 2008! I'm in for $100 if she sticks around."

This commentary is as telling about the lengths the GOP went to "keep Chafee" as it is about the state of the Republican Party today. Note to Karl Rove: When the only person eager to contribute to the NRSC is Moulitsas, you know the Republican Party is in trouble.

NO RISK, NO REWARD

Losing was a first for me. It came as a surprise, partly because the Chafee campaign was acting like they were twenty points behind and partly because it is the nature of campaigns to be single-mindedly focused on winning. We were preparing for victory up to the very last minute. With only seven weeks between primary day and the general election on November 7, there was no time to spare. We were ready to hit the ground running September 13, with a plan to be out at six-thirty the next morning waving to commuters at the busiest intersection in Rhode Island, Hoxie Four Corners.

Of course, we never made it to Hoxie Four Corners. Primary night, staff and close friends waited with me for the returns in a hotel room in Warwick's Crowne Plaza while supporters waited downstairs. At 9:03 p.m., three minutes after the polls closed, the all-knowing Fred received a call from a runner at a small Barrington precinct where a total of four hundred votes had been cast, and said, "Mayor, it's going to be tough. At best you win fifty-one to forty-nine." This was not a good sign; Fred had never been wrong before. At 10:20 p.m., with 80% of the vote in, I was behind by four thousand votes. It was over. In the end that margin held, and I lost 54–46. I called Senator Chafee, congratulated him, and told him that I would announce my support for his candidacy. This was in stark contrast to Chafee's refusal to support me had I won,[2] but so be it. I played little league baseball growing up, so I knew what to do. When you lose, you line up, shake hands, and say "Good luck" to the winning team. I was a Republican, even in defeat.

When I finally made it to the podium, surrounded by my family and friends, there was really nothing for me to say except "Thank you." My concession speech was an outpouring of gratitude to the real Republicans who made this campaign possible. These were people like Eddie–"You knocked on every door for four years, I love you"; Martha Stamp–"my number one fan" and a walking Laffey billboard; Billy and Harvey Bennett, my childhood heroes from across the street; my mom, who had just come out of knee surgery but wouldn't miss that night for the world–"I'm sorry Mom, I'll tell Dad tomorrow"; and Bruce Lane who had rented me the eight-by-eight room that served as our pre-headquarters. These were people who never stopped working and never stopped believing. They had Ronald Reagan's faith and optimism. I would take them over a million Liddy Doles any day.

Even at that moment, when I realized that the past twelve months had come to a grinding halt, there were no regrets. From the very beginning, I told my investors that we would raise $2 million and get thirty thousand people out to vote for me–unheard of in a Rhode Island Republican primary[3]–and we did. As I told my supporters that night, "Without taking any risk, there's really no reward; and we took a lot of risk, a lot of personal risk, a lot of professional risk to do what we did here this past year." This was especially true of those supporters who were members of local Republican committees. They assumed a great deal of personal and professional risk to support me and buck the establishment.

The national Republican leaders could have learned a thing or two from these folks. They could have learned something about the meaning of principle, and the courage that comes with taking principled risks. Instead, these so-called leaders thought they were playing it safe by supporting Chafee in the pursuit of power. They thought they were playing it safe with "comprehensive" immigration reform; they thought they were playing it safe by trying to co-opt the Democrats with No Child Left Behind; and they thought they were playing it safe when they passed a transportation bill pinker than Porky the Pig himself.

But this "low-risk" strategy ended up alienating all the grass-roots people I mentioned in my speech and millions more like them across Rhode Island and America. On September 13, 2006, in a postmortem editorial entitled "The Importance of Being a Laffey," the editors of the *National Review* wrote the next day: "Senators are a notoriously risk-averse crowd. And now, for the second election cycle in a row, Republican senators have received a sharp reminder that if they behave too much like liberals, they may not be senators for long."

"You get what you pay for," goes the popular adage. Nowhere was this more true than in Rhode Island. For too long, Republicans acted like Democrats. Now they got a Democratic majority.

LINC CHAFEE: A FAILED INVESTMENT

Lincoln Chafee was supposed to be the Republican Party's saving grace. He was supposed to ride into victory on both September 12 and November 7 on a shiny white horse, an apt metaphor given Chafee's penchant for equine creatures. But that's not exactly how things turned out. Thanks to the millions of dollars and the extensive get-out-the-vote effort he received from the national Republican Party, Chafee won on September 12 all right, but he wasted no time in throwing that victory in the party's face.

Shortly after the NRSC's Pyrrhic victory, Chafee maintained his opposition to John Bolton's nomination as U.S. ambassador to the United Nations. Bolton's recess appointment was due to expire on January 3, 2007, and with all the Democrats on the Senate Committee on Foreign Relations opposed to Bolton's nomination, Chafee held the key vote. Despite Bolton's stellar record in the United Nations over the past year, Chafee opposed his confirmation because he had "serious questions about this Administration's policies in the Middle East" and because he wanted to push for a "more balanced approach" in the Israeli-Palestinian conflict—whatever that means.

Over the following days, Chafee was also the only Republican to vote against a bill providing funds to build a fence along the U.S.-Mexico border, even though he claimed throughout the campaign that he supported increased border security. With eighty senators—twenty-six of whom were Democrats—supporting this bill, Linc Chafee once again found himself in the minority of the entire U.S. Senate. Incredibly, Chafee was also one of only four Republicans to vote against the Child Custody Protection Act, a bill that made it illegal for someone other than a parent to take a minor across state lines for an abortion. Linc Chafee may have won the Republican primary in Rhode Island, but it sure didn't make him a Republican.

As Chafee repeatedly thumbed his nose at the party, some in the establishment began to question what exactly the Republican Party had gained by supporting the wayward senator. According to the weekly conservative magazine *Human Events*, one anonymous senator asked: "What the NRSC did to a conservative candidate [Steve Laffey] was disgusting and unprecedented. But it's done, so why doesn't Liddy Dole call in the chit with Linc Chafee and get a vote on Bolton?" But the Washington Republicans never understood what Rhode Island Republicans knew instinctively: Linc Chafee was a principled Democrat.

In "The Importance of Being a Laffey," the editors wrote: "There's no special reason to believe that Chafee will even remain in the GOP: Two years ago, when *USA Today* asked him about switching parties, Chafee replied: 'I'm not ruling it out.' This man could be the next Jim Jeffords." Seven weeks later, these words proved eerily prophetic. Two days after he lost the general election to Sheldon Whitehouse, Chafee displayed his true colors once and for all. Standing in front of a throng of local reporters at his Providence office, a weary Chafee announced his pleasure with the Democrats' resounding victory, reiterated his opposition to Bolton, blamed me for his defeat, and—surprise, surprise—said he may not remain a Republican.

REPORTER: *Is it possible—and I'm not sure how to phrase this so I'll just try it straight—that by you giving the political equivalent of the ultimate sacrifice, you may have done something very important for the country— your losing, a few others losing, however people may have felt about you personally, may have done a good thing? Was that part of your thinking?*

CHAFEE: *Uh . . .*

REPORTER: *Saving lives, changing the course of the war?*

CHAFEE: *Yes, I know a lot of people are coming up to me today, saying, uh, that we're sorry you lost but we're glad the Congress switched.*

REPORTER: *Do you feel that way?*

CHAFEE: *Uh, to be honest, yes.*

REPORTER: *Are you considering becoming an Independent like Jeffords did? Are you considering making the huge switch and becoming a Democrat?*

CHAFEE: *Uh, I'm just recovering from a very difficult, bruising campaign, and haven't made any decisions. I just haven't even thought about where my place is.*

REPORTER: *But now, after Election Day, and it's all over, you're saying you're looking—kind of looking—where you belong, and it may not be the Republican Party?*

CHAFEE: *That's fair.*

A sitting U.S. senator who just lost his seat could say a lot of things. In fact, a lot of losing senators did. Rick Santorum urged his supporters to "give it up, give him a round of applause!" for his opponent, Bob Casey. George Allen wished his opponent, Jim Webb, well and "pledged to Jim Webb my absolute full cooperation in the transition." But no self-respecting member of the Republican Party would actually say they were happy the Democrats took control. But then again, Chafee announced that he may not be a Republican for long. He reiterated this point in a front-page *New York Times* article three weeks later, saying, "I'm caught between the state party, which I'm very comfortable in, and the national party, which I'm not," adding that he was weighing the idea of "sticking it out and hoping the pendulum swings back." Back to where? Back to Nelson Rockefeller, Gerald Ford, and the mantra of Whip Inflation Now?

To those of us who followed Chafee's hemming and hawing over the past seven years, his fickle behavior that November afternoon was par for the course. We still hadn't forgotten Chafee's 2004 admission to the *New York Times* that "he went to bed at night wondering how he could remain a Republican." We knew the only reason Chafee didn't switch parties in 2001 was that Jeffords had the guts to beat him to it, and the only reason he remained a Republican all these years was to benefit from the pork the party paid him to keep the "R" next to his name.[4] For those of us who said all these things back in September 2005 while the press laughed itself silly, there was a lot of vindication to go around. But there were was also a sense of "what if." What would have happened had the Republican Party recognized Chafee for the opportunist that he was? How would have things turned out differently if President Bush had put his foot down and said, "No. I can't support this guy. He has never supported this party"?

As a businessman who worked in the world of investment banking for fifteen years, I know a thing or two about making wise investments. There are several factors you want to take into account. One: How much money, time, or effort will you be investing in said project? Two: What are the chances of seeing a return on that investment? Three: How large will that return be? And four: Are there any potentially negative side effects—exogenous variables as we say in the economics world—of this investment?

As I listened to the soon-to-be-ex-senator Chafee's press conference, I wondered if Karl Rove and the president actually sat down to discuss these four basic questions. I was forced to conclude that the answer was no, because if they had, there is no possible way they could have taken the actions they did.

Let us, for a moment, imagine what that conversation would have sounded like:

ROVE: *That's the story in Pennsylvania. Now on to Rhode Island. Laffey announced he's running, and we have to decide exactly what we want to do about it. We have a couple of choices, Mr. President. We could do nothing—just stay out of it. We can go the Toomey-Specter route and just support the incumbent. Or we can do something we've never done before—what Senator Dole is strongly recommending—going nuclear negative on Steve Laffey and getting the liberals out to vote for Chafee. That's probably the only way Chafee could win the primary.*

BUSH: *All right, Karl, let's think this thing through. What can we do to support Chafee without attacking this Laffey fellow?*

ROVE: *Uh . . . interesting question, Mr. President. Not much policywise. Chafee disagrees with us on pretty much everything, except free trade. Not sure that's a winning issue up in Rhode Island. We could run fluff pieces on Chafee's character, independence, et cetera.*

BUSH: *Or we could run up the negatives on Laffey. What could we say—doesn't he agree with us on most things?*

ROVE: *I've got Senator Dole's people working on the opposition research as we speak. It would be mostly character stuff—attack him personally, see if we can dig up anything on the family—that kind of stuff.*

BUSH: *What happens if we go the negative route, but Chafee loses—either the primary or the general? How much wasted money are we talking about? What about our donors? A lot of those folks think Chafee's a liberal, and between you and me, Karl, they're right.*

ROVE: *Good questions, Mr. President. The money will depend on how well Laffey fund-raises and whether the Club for Growth enters the picture, but let's assume worst-case scenario—it could be a lot of money. A couple million. Rhode Island's a cheap market, but Chafee is not a skilled fund-raiser, and, well, he's kind of a dull fellow. Not very good on the campaign trail. And if I had to put money down, I'd bet the Club for Growth jumps into the fray. Toomey won't be able to resist. Honestly, my gut says Chafee will need a lot of help.*

BUSH: *And our supporters? The base? Our donors? They're not that happy with some of the things we've done recently—No Child Left Behind, campaign finance, the transportation bill . . . I'm concerned we may be pressing our luck.*

ROVE: *You'd have to tell them that control of the Senate depends on this election.*

BUSH: *But what about other close races around the country—Talent, Santorum, Burns, and that Maryland fellow—what's his name . . . Steele—these folks could benefit from the money we would spend on Chafee, and to be honest, Karl, I'd rather have them in the Senate than Chafee. And don't think I've forgotten about that drug comment back in '99. What are the polls on those other races?*

ROVE: *The latest Rasmussen poll has Talent at a literal dead heat. Burns is up by thirteen. Strategic Vision has Santorum down by eleven, and Steele is down by five points—could be a real opportunity to make headway in Maryland.*

BUSH: *What about Tennessee?*

ROVE: *Ford is up by a couple of points—not a good sign.*

BUSH: *Wouldn't it make more sense to put our resources into these races? Even if we pour millions into Chafee's campaign and he wins, all we get from him is the caucus vote. On everything else—tax cuts, judges—he's with the Democrats. And what if the Senate is 50-50? Who's to say Chafee won't pull a Jeffords? He's not loyal to the party, Karl—I can see it in his eyes. He'd switch at the first opportunity. I don't trust the guy.*

ROVE: *These are all very good points, Mr. President, but Senator Dole feels very strongly that we need to stick to our tradition of supporting incumbents.*

BUSH: *But we don't have a tradition of attacking fellow Republicans!*

ROVE: *True, but our support won't be worth anything unless we take Laffey down. Listen, do you want me to bring Senator Dole in? Maybe if you went over the particulars with her, maybe if she shows you the polling we did on Laffey and Chafee—*

BUSH: *No. We've never attacked another Republican before, especially not in defense of a liberal like Chafee, and I'm not going to start now. It just doesn't make sense. We run the risk of wasting millions of dollars that could be better spent on better seats, pissing off key supporters, and a Jeffords situation. It's not smart politics. Tell Senator Dole I've made my decision, and it's final. Now get me some of that pecan pie, Karl. All this strategizing makes a guy awfully hungry.*

Of course, that's not how it happened at all. In the end, Linc Chafee proved to be the most spectacularly failed investment of the 2006 election cycle. Writing two days after the primary, Jeanne Cummings of the *Wall Street Journal* asked: "The Republican Party leadership won the primary battle in Rhode Island, getting their preferred candidate, incumbent Sen. Lincoln Chafee, past a conservative challenger. But at what cost?"

By November 7, the answer to that question was very clear and it was not pretty. Investing in Chafee cost the party millions in potential contributions triggered by grassroots anger. The same investment cost the party money and time spent in Rhode Island that would have been better used elsewhere. Recall that Republicans lost the Senate by one seat. The "electable" Chafee did not come close to keeping his, but three Republican seats were lost by razor-thin margins: George Allen by 1 percent in Virginia; Conrad Burns by 1 percent in Montana; and Jim Talent by 3 percent in Missouri. Would the extra money or manpower have been enough to put Allen over the top and keep the Senate in Republican hands? I guess we'll never know, but it seems like an awful shame if you ask me. All that money, all that time, all for a guy who took his thumb and shoved it right in your eye.

CHAPTER 10

A Prescription for the Future

"One of the great paradoxes in politics is that governing to maintain power is the surest way to lose it. Republicans have the ideas to solve our greatest challenges. If we focus on ideas, our majority status will take care of itself."
—Senator Tom Coburn, November 8, 2006

THE MORNING AFTER

Wednesday, November 8, 2006, Republicans across the country woke to the nauseating picture of Nancy Pelosi embracing Chuck Schumer. The results of the November 7 elections were as bad as the polls predicted, if not worse. The House went solidly Democratic with a thirty-seat pickup, and the Senate followed suit as Conrad Burns went down in Montana and Virginia's George Allen conceded two days later. The ultimate nightmare became a reality played out on the national stage: Speaker of the House Nancy Pelosi; Majority Leader Harry Reid; House Majority Leader Steny Hoyer.

As the Monday-morning quarterbacking began in earnest, it was clear that the wave that brought the Republicans to power in 1994 had run its course. But what had taken its place? Was this a Democratic revolution twelve years after the Republican version? Was Nancy Pelosi the new Newt Gingrich of 2006? Was a liberal revolution on the brink of capturing American hearts and minds?

Even as Republicans grappled with the question of what happened, it was clear that the answer to the above questions was no, no, and no! The Republicans won in 1994 because they offered the country a compelling alternative to the liberalism of the past generation. With Newt Gingrich at the helm, the Contract with America called for fiscal responsibility in the form of a balanced budget, personal responsibility in the form of welfare reform, and the restoration of the American Dream in the form of major tax relief. Republicans won because they offered the country a specific plan and a positive vision for America. And they won big, claiming fifty-four House seats and eight in the Senate. Unlike the 2006 midterm elections, in which many Republicans were defeated by razor-thin margins, Republicans were ushered into Congress in 1994 by overwhelming majorities on a platform of real change.

The 2006 election was entirely different. Chuck Schumer's and Nancy Pelosi's beaming faces to the contrary, the Democrats didn't actually win. The Republicans lost. The Democrats didn't offer any compelling ideas or alternatives; they merely pointed out over and over again where and how the Republicans had messed up. The Republican-controlled Congress and the Bush administration gave the Democrats too much ammunition, and the Democrats were smart enough to use it. As an angry blogger on Red State (www.redstate.com) put it: "The Democrats did not win this battle. We locked our finest spears in the ground and plunged ourselves upon them."

Republicans lost, but Republican ideas did not lose. To be sure, the Democratic Party of 2006 was spearheaded by left-wingers like Nancy Pelosi, Chuck Schumer, and Howard Dean, but the Democrats won by putting up candidates who sounded an awful lot like Republicans. Jim Webb of Virginia was a Reagan Republican turned Democrat who served as Reagan's secretary of the navy and continues to harbor deep dislike for Jimmy Carter and Bill Clinton. In Pennsylvania, the same Democratic Party that refused to allow the pro-life Pennsylvania governor Bob Casey to speak at the 1992 Democratic Convention in New York happily embraced his pro-life son, Bob Casey Jr., to oppose Rick Santorum. And Harold Ford Jr. in Tennessee opposed gay marriage and late-term abortions, and was even named by Ann Coulter as "one of my favorite Democrats." Ultimately, Democrats won by stifling their inherent liberal instincts in order to keep Reagan Democrats in line, and Republicans lost by failing to give the Republicans and right-of-center Independents a reason to come out in droves.

Of course, the talking heads saw things a little bit differently. No two ways about it, the 2006 election cycle was proof positive that the GOP had moved too far to the right. If Republicans wanted to maintain a viable political party, they had to become, in the words of Pennsylvania senator Arlen Specter, "a lot more progressive and a lot less ideological." Bill Schneider of CNN chimed in, claiming that "Republicans lost because they abandoned the center." But if anything, the 2006 elections showed just the opposite. In his first six years as president, Bush moved to the middle on a number of fronts, but his less-than-subtle attempts at triangulation failed to garner any love from the left, the center, or the right. Bush abandoned Republican principles on No Child Left Behind, Medicare Part D, border security, and spending. None of these endeared him to the left, and they certainly didn't endear him to his base on the right.

Bush tried to be too much to too many, thinking that the path to victory lay in tossing out as many bones as possible. Reagan understood this pitfall better than anyone else. At a Washington conference in March 1975 convened to discuss the future of the party, President Gerald Ford argued that the party "needed to expand ideologically in order to be viable," writes Craig Shirley in *Reagan's Revolution*. But when it came time for Reagan to speak, he urged the Republican Party "to stand for one thing to all people and not try to be all things to all people."

BODY BLOWS

Imagine the following scenario: You're taking a cross-country trip from California to Massachusetts in your brand-spanking-new Ford F-150 pickup truck. You're cruising through Death Valley with the music blaring in the background when you notice the air conditioner is just not keeping you cool. *Ah, those darn four cylinders,* you think. *They just don't make air conditioners like they used to.* As you approach Colorado, you hear a rattle in the back right door. When you stop for gas, you jiggle the door and wonder, *What the heck is going on? It's a brand-new car.* In the back of your mind, you know something is just not right, but you turn the music up and try to ignore it. In Chicago, the muffler starts clattering right below you. You're annoyed, but you don't want to give up on the car. You just bought it a couple of weeks ago! Somewhere in upstate New York, when only one headlight works as you're twisting along the country roads in near pitch blackness, you know . . . you know you bought a lemon. But you don't want to admit it, and you don't want to tell your wife because she wanted a Honda—*you* insisted on the F-150. By the time you get to Massachusetts, all four wheels have come off. Folks, that's where we are today—on a shoulder on the Massachusetts Turnpike, all four wheels off the car. And here's your choice: Remove the vehicle identification numbers, torch the car, and move on—or patch it up and hobble along.

I say: Torch the car.

Over the past six years, the Republican base suffered one body blow after another, and anyone who's watched professional boxing knows, the human body can only sustain so many blows before it falls unconscious. Whether it was No Child Left Behind or Medicare Part D, these body blows came in different forms but they were all violations of fundamental Republican principles, and they all played a role in the disastrous results of November 7, 2006.

The 2006 midterms were the equivalent of the wheels falling off the car, but there was plenty of evidence of problems along the way. My race in Rhode Island was the final embodiment of these problems, but there were other major warning signs. For whatever reason, Republicans chose not to heed those warnings. Maybe we were simply too comfortable with our positions of power. Maybe we dismissed each body blow as an aberration or the price of getting Republican candidates reelected. Maybe we knew that something was terribly wrong, but we just didn't want to admit it out loud.

There are a lot of fingers to point, and no doubt President Bush and the Republican Congress deserve a lot of the blame, but ultimately we are responsible for our own fate. Where were the outcries when the school choice plan that George W. Bush campaigned on in 2000 became a massive federal intervention into the local school system? Where was the indignation when Republican members of Congress turned appropriation bills into pork-filled goody bags for their friends? The first time we truly saw grassroots outrage was when President Bush picked Harriet Miers to fill Sandra Day O'Connor's Supreme Court seat. And look what happened. We ended up with something a whole lot better: We got Sam Alito. This was the perfect example of our responsibility as grassroots Republicans. More important, it was the perfect example of what we are capable of accomplishing when we decide to stand up for the principles we believe in. Unlike the Harriet Miers nomination, the body blows that I list below did not arouse the same level of anger and passion, if any at all. For every single one of these blows, it was our job to stand up, stick our heads out the window, and yell, much like Howard Beale in the 1976 movie *Network*: "I'm as mad as hell and I'm not going to take this anymore!"

BODY BLOW #1:
NO DEMOCRAT LEFT BEHIND

Democrats have long owned the issue of education. A 1996 Gallup poll found 44 percent of respondents thought the Democratic Party was more interested in improving public education, compared with 27 percent of respondents who chose the Republican Party. In 1998, this education gap remained strong: 39 percent chose the Democrats compared with the Republicans' 27 percent.

These numbers should not come as a surprise. After all, it was Jimmy Carter who created the Department of Education, and it was Ronald Reagan who campaigned in 1980 on abolishing it. As late as 1996, the Republican Party Platform declared the Department of Education unconstitutional and pledged to "abolish the Department of Education, end federal meddling in our schools, and promote family choice at all levels of learning."

Four years later, under the banner of compassionate conservatism, George W. Bush resolved to change those numbers. Though he denied knowing what triangulation meant, he managed to do just that, co-opting the issue of education and putting a Republican spin on it. At stump speech after stump speech, he spoke about "the bigotry of low expectations" and school choice, declaring in his 2000 national convention speech: "When a school district receives federal funds to teach poor children, we expect them to learn. And if they don't, parents should get the money to make a different choice."

But then Bush got elected, and instead of hearing about vouchers and parental choice, we started hearing about increased federal control, national standardized testing, and Ted Kennedy.

At the beginning of his first term, Bush's $47.6 billion five-year plan included a modest voucher proposal that would grant parents of students in failing schools $1,500 to put toward private school tuition. But as Bush met with Ted Kennedy and other like-minded senators, voucher proponents began to question the president's commitment to the one true aspect of reform in the No Child Left Behind bill. When Ted Kennedy says, "There are some areas of difference, but the overwhelming areas of agreement and of support are very, very powerful," nine times out of ten, that's a very bad sign. Make that ten out of ten.

By May, the voucher program was dead. On May 2, 2001, the House Education Committee voted 27–20, including five Republicans, to kill the program, leaving conservatives on the Hill grumbling about what was now essentially a Democratic bill, or as the Heritage Foundation labeled it, "an expensive version of the status quo." With vouchers stripped from the bill, No Child Left Behind was simply a massive federal program with testing mandates that stripped schools of local control and increased federal spending on education by 48 percent over the next three years. "When the President talked about reform," Representative Jim DeMint of South Carolina told the *National Review*, "we didn't realize he intended to 'Leave No Democrats Behind.' "

A few principled Republicans—such as DeMint and John Shadegg of Arizona—aside, the overwhelming majority of Republican legislators accepted this first body blow without so much as a whimper. On December 13, 2001, the House voted 348–41 to approve the No Child Left Behind Act of 2001, and the Senate gave its stamp of approval by an overwhelming 87–10 five days later. To be fair, Senator Judd Gregg of New Hampshire introduced a very mild trial vouchers program as an amendment on the floor, but even this trial program was defeated 58–41, with eleven Republicans (Chafee included) joining with the Democrats to squash it.

At the time, Republicans were overjoyed by the gains they had made in the public's perception on education. With No Child Left Behind, Bush had closed the decades-long gap between Democrats and Republicans on the issue. In April 2001, three polls had Republicans outscoring Democrats, and this alone was reason enough for most Republicans—many of whom won political office campaigning on smaller government—to support the final No Child Left Behind product, no matter what it looked like. As Representative Bob Schaffer explained in May 2001, "The Republicans want a political win."

But by 2004, this so-called political win had become an albatross as Democrats regained their double-digit lead on education. Even liberal Democrats like Ted Kennedy—one of the chief architects of this disaster—distanced himself from the results of NCLB, blaming Republicans for not going far enough. Now there's a familiar refrain: If a government program doesn't work, it must be because it didn't go far enough.

Worse, five years after Bush signed No Child Left Behind, the bill failed to accomplish what it set out to do. According to a report by the Civil Rights Project at Harvard University, as reported in the *Wall Street Journal*, NCLB "did not have a significant impact on overall test scores and has not narrowed the racial and socio-economic achievement gap" over the four years since its implementation. Nor has the modest choice element remaining in NCLB been applied. Although Congress stripped NCLB of private school choice, it allowed students in failing public schools to transfer to other public schools, even outside their district. The Government Accountability Office reported that only 1 percent of all students eligible for public school choice in 2002–2003 had transferred to new schools. One of the major reasons for these paltry results is that schools failed to notify parents of the option in a timely manner or, in some cases, at all.

A mere five years after Republicans argued for abolishing the Department of Education, Republicans happily accepted a massive federal encroachment into local education that will, it seems, never end. As the bill comes up for renewal this year, Democrats like Ted Kennedy predictably argue that we need to pour "more resources" into schools. Nothing could be further from the truth.

Clearly what we need is not more of the same but something entirely different.

BODY BLOW #2: D FOR DUMB

Medicare Part D was another example of Republicans trying to act like Democrats in order to win elections. Much like No Child Left Behind, this massive new federal program was heralded as a mark of genius, described by a *Christian Science Monitor* reporter as a "political stroke worthy of Bill Clinton." "Mr. Bush had just picked the Democrats' pocket," the reporter continued. "Never mind that many voters have lingering questions about Bush's $400 billion move to add a prescription-drug benefit to Medicare. The issue is off the table, leaving Democrats to argue over the scraps."

Unfortunately, all short-term political wins come to an end when the reality of the mess created begins to sink in. And what a mess it is. As is often the case with new federal entitlement programs, there were a lot of noble intentions to go around. Back in 2003, Republicans faced a real problem: some seniors could not afford to buy prescription drugs, hiking up the cost of Medicare and practically handing Democrats a cudgel and a permission slip to beat the Republicans up with it. But these seniors represented a small sector of the country's senior population, many of whom were covered by private employee plans or Medicaid. Instead of targeting these seniors directly, the Republican-controlled Congress created a massive new entitlement program covering all seniors, costing a whopping $678 billion over ten years and totaling 1,162 pages in regulatory minutiae. According to the *New York Times*, an estimated 3.8 million seniors will be moved out of their perfectly working prescription drug plans into what can only be described as a bureaucratic nightmare worthy of Dante's Inferno. Talk about trying to fix a machine that isn't broken by breaking it.

What was so devastating to grassroots Republicans was that

Medicare Part D was so clearly a violation of tried-and-true principles in favor of a quick political win. Today, Republicans have neither a win nor a sustainable policy to show for their sacrifice. Instead, the party of small government has created another government behemoth and another opportunity for Democrats to argue that the best way to fix the broken machine is to bulk it up with more parts. During the 2006 election cycle, Democratic candidates campaigned *against* Medicare Part D, arguing that it did not go far enough. This is what Republicans have to look forward to. The argument over whether a new entitlement program was necessary or wise is now over. The Democrats won that debate when the Republicans ceded it to them. The Republicans may have gained a couple of points in the 2004 election cycle, but they have lost something so much bigger: credibility with grassroot Republicans on controlling government spending.

BODY BLOW #3: OINK, OINK

On March 27, 1987, Ronald Reagan vetoed an $87.5 billion transportation bill that contained 152 pork-barrel projects, calling it "a textbook example of special-interest, pork-barrel politics at work." In 2002, grassroots Republicans hoped for a repeat when Bush included a picture of a wind-powered ice sled in his 2003 budget as an example of the kind of wasteful pork projects he refused to tolerate and declared: "Congressional earmarks undercut the [Transportation] Department's ability to fund projects that have successfully proved their merits."[1] Fast-forward to three years later. On August 10, 2005, Bush signed a $286 billion transportation bill, containing a record 6,371 pork projects, costing more than $24 billion, and announced to his audience in Montgomery, Illinois: "I'm proud to be here to sign this transportation bill."

Pork-barrel projects are specific line items written into appropriation bills that direct taxpayer dollars toward generally wasteful projects that serve a small segment of the population. These earmarks tend to be anonymous and slipped into bills at the last minute in closed-door committee meetings, often to reward political contributors and assure politicians a smooth path to reelection. When members of Congress vote on these bills, they often have no idea what kind of ridiculous projects they are voting for. And even if they do know, they are unwilling to take a stand, lest their own pet projects face rejection in retaliation.

The result? Over the past ten years, government greed has ballooned out of control and the number of pork projects dispensed on the backs of taxpayers has ballooned right along with it. Though Republicans were swept into office in 1994 on a platform of small government, they, too, fell under the spell that power wields so dangerously. The transportation bill is merely the most notable of the spending bills, but members of Congress stuff all thirteen appropriations bills to the brim with every kind of pet project imaginable. In 1996, the total number of pork projects emanating from federal spending bills was 958. By the time we got to the summer of 2005, that number had reached 13,997, or nearly fifteen times the 1996 number.

Congress defends these pork projects to the death, claiming that they are vital and appropriate uses of your tax dollars. Oh really? Let's take a look at some of these critical projects:

- $5.8 million to the Vermont Association of Snow Travelers for a snowmobile trail.

- $900,000 for the Washington, D.C., Shakespeare Theatre.

- $2 million for a parking lot at the privately owned University of the Incarnate Word.

- $950,000 for Philadelphia's Please Touch Museum.

- $1.85 million for a viticulture consortium at Cornell University.

I will spare you a list of all thirteen thousand projects, but one more deserves mentioning. The most outrageous project of 2005 was, hands down, Alaska's Bridge to Nowhere, a $223 million line item to build a bridge to connect the Alaskan town of Ketchikan (population 8,900) to its airport on the Island of Gravina (population 50). At the time, residents of either town could make the trip via a ferry service at a price of $6 per car.

The proud father of this pork project was Alaska's seven-term Republican senator, Ted Stevens, a notorious porker responsible for Alaska's number one status as the recipient of the most pork per capita for at least the past seven years. In 2005, Alaskan residents each received $984.85 per person in federal pork, according to Citizens Against Government Waste. No state came close to this kind of per capita bounty. Even the second-place District of Columbia and third-place Hawaii each brought in half the per capita amount of pork at $464.61 and $454.47, respectively. If you live in Alaska, this might make you very happy. But if you live anywhere else, you should ask yourself why Alaskan residents are feeding off of your tax dollars, especially if you live in the state of Texas, where you're only getting $2.90 per person in pork projects.

When I took Chafee to task during the campaign for voting for the Bridge to Nowhere, he claimed that he had no choice because the Bridge to Nowhere was part of the larger transportation bill and he didn't have the option of voting against the bridge alone. Simply put, this was hogwash.

In October 2005, Senator Tom Coburn (R-OK) introduced an amendment to the transportation bill that would have transferred

$223 million from the Bridge to Nowhere to rebuild a bridge in Louisiana damaged by Hurricane Katrina. This seemed like a no-brainer, but I guess 85 percent of the U.S. Senate thought otherwise, because only fifteen U.S. senators voted for Coburn's amendment. Clearly, they didn't have the guts. They knew that a courageous stand against pork-barrel spending would throw their own pork projects into harm's way, and how would they get re-elected if they had nothing to tout and wave come November?

According to the *New York Times*, Senator Patty Murray (D-WA) eloquently defended the $223 million Bridge to Nowhere. "I tell my colleagues, if we start cutting funding for individual projects, your project may be next," Murray warned, threatening to take "a long, serious look" at the projects of those who voted against the bridge. Ted Stevens even threatened to resign if his precious bridge was stricken from the transportation bill. I don't know what Congress was thinking—Stevens's threat alone would have secured my vote.

If there was ever any shame in spending taxpayer dollars on ridiculous pet projects, that sentiment has gone the way of the dodo. "I happen to be a supporter of earmarks, unabashed," Senator Tom Harkin (D-IA) told the *New York Times*. Senator Robert Byrd of West Virginia, anointed the "King of Pork" by Citizens Against Government Waste, accurately summed up the overwhelming congressional attitude when he snapped, "You may as well slap my wife as take away my transportation funding." Of course, this was the same guy who used his heavyweight status on the Appropriations Committee to secure a Coast Guard facility for his noncoastal state.

If the arrogant waste of taxpayer dollars is not enough to persuade our congressional leaders from swearing off pork, perhaps the increasing number of pork-related corruption charges will do the trick. Exhibit A: California's former Republican representative Randy "Duke" Cunningham resigned in November 2005 after pleading guilty to taking $2.4 million in bribes from defense contractors who were dutifully rewarded with congressional earmarks. He sits today in a federal penitentiary. Perhaps he will soon have some company.

Representative Allan Mollohan (D-WV), ironically a ranking member of the House Ethics Committee until he was forced to step down, is currently under federal investigation for possibly "steering $250 million in federal earmarks to five nonprofit organizations staffed by his former aides and business partner," according to the *Wall Street Journal*. Much like his fellow West Virginian, Senator Byrd, Mollohan has long been a defender of congressional pork. When questioned about allegations of misconduct in 2005, he responded: "All I care about is supporting companies and [federal] programs that companies are doing in my Congressional district." Nearly two hundred years after our Founding Fathers warned of overreaching, we are witnessing the sad fulfillment of James Monroe's 1822 prediction, in which he argued that federal funds should be limited "to national works only since if it were unlimited it would be liable to abuse and might be productive of evil."

President Bush's mistake was that he didn't do anything. He rolled over and played dead while the Republican-controlled Congress ran roughshod over its own principles. There is a reason why the Founding Fathers gave the president of the United States the power to veto legislation, and you don't need to look much further than the 2005 transportation bill to find it. In fact, eighty appropriation bills have suffered a presidential veto since the veto was first inaugurated by George Washington in 1792. The transportation bill of 2005 should have been the eighty-first.

Sometimes leaders think they will be measured by what they did, and not by what they did not do. This is a mistake. Often it is the lack of bold, decisive action that is the most fatal blow of all.

BODY BLOW #4: COMPREHENSIVE IMMIGRATION REFORM, MY FOOT

Throughout my race I told reporters that I could not think of one issue where there was a bigger disconnect between what the Washington elites were doing and what the regular folks were demanding than on the issue of immigration. Poll after poll demonstrated that voters viewed illegal immigration as a serious problem and supported an enforcement-first strategy. Even in Rhode Island— just about as far as you can get from the Mexican border—68 percent favored enforcement first, according to a Rasmussen poll.

Much as they did with No Child Left Behind, Americans knew they were in trouble on immigration when Bush teamed up with Ted Kennedy and John McCain to produce the McCain-Kennedy bill. This bill was touted as a compromise bill by its supporters. In other words, instead of granting amnesty to all illegal aliens currently in the country (as Chafee and Diane Feinstein wanted to do), it granted amnesty to *almost* all illegal aliens, excepting illegal aliens residing in America two years or less. To add insult to injury, the McCain-Kennedy bill guaranteed foreign construction workers higher wages than American employees working in the same industry. I have a feeling that the roofers I met in Smithfield—along with their fellow construction workers all across America—had some colorful words to say about that.

The one thing Bush forgot to take into account is that the American people are smart. They're willing to make a mistake once, but not more than that. They tried amnesty in 1986, and they didn't like what they saw. Even Ronald Reagan's own advisers urged Congress not to retravel that road. In a December 2006 column for *Human Events*, Reagan's attorney general, Ed Meese, who oversaw Reagan's 1986 amnesty plan, acknowledged that "the lesson from the 1986 experience is that such an amnesty did not solve the problem." "What would President Reagan do?" Meese asked. "For one thing, he would not repeat the mistakes of the past, including those of his own administration."

Amnesty is a quick fix with far-reaching consequences that helps neither America nor our impoverished neighbors south of the border. The only people who stand to gain from the Senate's amnesty bill are the Democrats hoping to pick up a new pool of Hispanic voters and Republicans eager to keep their big-business friends happy. But the losers in this political game are the people who can least afford it: the working-class Americans who are losing jobs to illegal aliens; the school systems that can't assimilate such large influxes of alien children; legal immigrants who came to this country the hard way; Hispanics waiting their turn on the other side of the border; women placing their life savings and bodies into the hands of coyotes (human traffickers) who make a living off of exploiting the vulnerable; and poor Hispanics trapped in impoverished countries that have no incentive to change as long as money keeps flowing in from America.

Finally, it is the country as a whole that stands to lose the most from a debate that has focused on immigration and not on the massive national security threat posed by our porous border and a Mexican mafia eager to make a quick buck delivering anonymous customers onto American soil. To be sure, there are major immigration issues that need to be dealt with, mostly by enforcing the laws already on the books, but the real questions are these: Six years after 9/11, why haven't the president and Congress secured our borders? Democratic and Republican politicians alike claim they support measures to secure our borders, so why don't they stop yakking and just do it already?

BODY BLOW #5: OVERWHELMING INCOMPETENCE

No honest discussion of the 2006 election cycle can be had without at least a brief mention of the Republican Party's overwhelming incompetence over the past couple of years. Whether it was its policies in Iraq, the administration's handling of Hurricane Katrina, the failure to enact a national energy plan, or the party's silence in the face of corruption among its own ranks, the Republican Party failed its base not only on principles but also on its ability, or inability as the case may be, to govern.

This is not a book about whether we should have invaded Iraq or how the administration should have handled Hurricane Katrina, but a primer for the Republican Party of the future. If Republicans want to win elections, they need to demonstrate that they have not only the ideas with which to govern but also the ability to do so.

PRESCRIPTION FOR THE FUTURE

Solutions happen when our leaders put long-term gains ahead of short-term wins. Because our leaders down in Washington are having difficulty grasping this message, let me explain it to them the same way I explain it to the kids in the Cranston school system: When I was growing up, I used to sit at my desk in my room studying every night. My buddies drove by, pulled up outside my bedroom window, and yelled, "Laffey, dude!" Now, it would have been a lot more fun to ditch the books and hang out with them, but I needed to go to college, so I sat there and did my calculus homework.

Many of the problems we face in this country require long-term solutions. Quick political fixes make for good commercials come election time, but they make for lousy governing. During my campaign, the only politician I heard who got it right was Senator Tom Coburn of Oklahoma, who sat next to me at the National Federation of Republican Assemblies meeting in Rhode Island and said, and I paraphrase, "I'm here to put America first; Oklahoma comes second."

Politicians are so worried about their own political futures they forget to worry about the future of the country. They need to stop worrying about winning and start offering long-term solutions that work. They need to stop acting like Democrats and start acting like Reagan Republicans. Is it risky? Sure. But they need to have a little faith in the American people. We're a lot smarter than they give us credit for.

EDUCATION–SCHOOL CHOICE IS THE ONLY CHOICE

Bush's triangulation on education was the first step toward strangulation. If Republicans want to regain the public's confidence on education, they need to offer solutions that have a track record of success. The federal government has thrown taxpayer dollars at the public school system over the past fifty years, and the public school system just gets worse. In contrast, voucher programs have sprung up in states all across the country, and the results are startlingly good.

The idea for vouchers was born in 1955 when Nobel laureate Milton Friedman argued that parents should be allowed to choose the school that best fits their children's needs. Over half a century later, various voucher programs exist in Ohio; Wisconsin; Washington, D.C.; Florida; Utah; Maine; Arizona; and Vermont. The most famous of these is Milwaukee's Parental Choice Program, started in 1990 and expanded further in 1995, in which eligible low-income students in Milwaukee's public schools are given a voucher worth up to $5,943 (in 2004–2005) to put toward private school tuition.

Numerous studies have demonstrated that these voucher programs result in improved test scores among participants as well as improvements in test scores for students in public schools exposed to voucher competition. The list of these studies is long,[2] and kudos to the academics turning out these numbers, but it's kind of like saying, "Let's do another study to see if smoking is bad for you." We don't need reams of academic reports; we just need a little common sense. More competition drives prices down and quality of service up. Oh, and smoking is bad for you.

The Republican Party is supposed to be the party of free markets, but it has done an awfully poor job of communicating this philosophy over the past six years. The free market allows for competition because it allows for choice. Right now, parents have no choice. Our current education system takes square pegs and attempts to shove them into round holes. Any parent knows that all of our children are different. My own five children are different from one another. Some have been educated in public schools, some in private schools. My oldest son alone has been educated in a number of different types of schools depending on his needs at the various stages of his education. Now, my wife and I are blessed. We have the assets to make the decisions that are best for our children, but not everyone is so fortunate. Voucher programs allow all parents the freedom to make the best education choices for their children.

Finally, the political advantages of school choice are as good as the practical advantages. The National Educational Association (NEA) aside, Americans, especially in minority communities, are huge fans of voucher programs. Poll after poll demonstrates that this is true,[3] as does my own personal experience.

When I campaigned in South Providence, a poor, mostly minority area with all the public schools in the area labeled failing, I found smart, intelligent people on this issue. I told folks in South Providence the same story I told wealthier folks in Barrington. Principles don't change just because the zip code does:

> *Ma'am, if we walk off these steps and you break your leg, we don't take you around the corner to some quack named Bob who had only one year of medical school just because you live on New York Avenue. We take you to Rhode Island Hospital. But because you live in this area and the only public school nearby is a failing one, your children are stuck in lousy schools. Wouldn't you rather get a check to help you send them to a better school of your choice?*

I never met anyone who thought this was a bad idea, but then again I didn't bump into Linc Chafee or the head of the NEA while I was knocking on doors in South Providence. Some people talk about wedge issues. This is the ultimate wedge issue, separating limousine liberals like Linc Chafee and Ted Kennedy, who send their kids to private schools but deny poor minorities the same opportunity, from the people who keep voting for them. But let's not just drive a wedge between these groups; let's drive a tractor trailer.

HEALTH CARE–TRUST AMERICA

Instead of creating a massive new federal entitlement program, Republicans could have addressed the segment of seniors without prescription drug plans by offering them direct subsidies. This would have silenced the Democrats and allowed Republicans to move forward on the issue of health care using a traditional but proven Republican principle, namely, that the free market works.

In a 1999 interview, Al Gore said that, when faced with tough decisions, he asks himself, "What would Jesus do?" Now, I'm a big fan of Jesus, but when I have to make tough policy decisions, I open up Milton Friedman's book *Free to Choose* and say: "What would Friedman do?" Friedman would have said: "Let's adopt the Health Care Freedom Plan—free to choose your own health care." The Health Care Freedom Plan contains three parts:

1. Lower the cost of prescription drugs by allowing Americans to buy the same drugs at lower prices from other Western countries, as is done in Europe today through a process known as parallel trading. In Europe, there are companies that search out low-cost drugs in Italy; buy them up in large quantities at, say, $2.00 a pop; ship them to Denmark; slap a Spanish label over the Italian label; ship them to Spain; and sell them for $2.50, saving everyone money and making a profit. I guess even this simple arbitrage is too difficult for Congress to grasp, because the United States currently bans free trade when it comes to prescription drugs, even though drugs in other advanced countries are 50 percent cheaper.

Unfortunately, it was a Republican-controlled Senate that refused to allow parallel trading in the Medicare Part D bill under the notion that European and Canadian drugs aren't safe, as if people all over Ottawa are dropping dead. A more likely explanation can be found in a letter circulated by the drug lobby urging Congress to put the kibosh on parallel trading. If you ask me, the only safety concerns plaguing our congressional leaders were those pertaining to their own jobs and wallets.

2. Encourage Americans to control their own health care choices and costs by implementing health savings accounts. HSAs are basically 401(k) plans for health insurance. Employers and individuals deposit money in a health care account that the individual draws from during the year to pay for his health care costs. If the individual doesn't use that money, he gets to keep it and the interest accumulates. The reason HSAs work is that they force people to start paying attention to costs. This basic law of economics is really a basic law of human behavior: if people don't have to pay for a product or service out of their own pockets, they have no reason to worry about the cost. When HMOs or employers foot the bill, we assume it doesn't matter whether we really need a certain drug or medical test. After all, someone else is paying for it. The problem with this thinking is that we all pay into the insurance pool through higher premiums that continue to increase as the cost of health care increases. Health savings accounts force people to ask: How much is that MRI? Or: Can I have the generic version of that drug? In other words, HSAs force people to ask for the same service but at a lower price.

When I heard Bush talk about health savings accounts in his 2005 State of the Union speech, I thought he was serious about it. So when I negotiated three major union contracts in the city of Cranston where public sector unions had ruled by the sword, I initiated pro-consumer 401(k) health care plans as part of the contract as an option for our employees. I thought every Republican governor and mayor across the country was doing the same thing. Boy, was I surprised to find out that Cranston was the only municipality in all of New England to take this step.

If you listen to the liberal pundits, they'll tell you that only "the wealthy and healthy" are interested in HSAs, but city workers in Cranston who average $45,000 a year in income—the Teamsters, the International Laborers, the International Brotherhood of Police Officers—all thought it was a good idea when we explained it to them.

3. Allow all Americans the right to buy health insurance the way they buy life insurance: anywhere they want and from whom they want. Currently, federal and state laws forbid companies from offering employees health insurance plans out of state. This is a serious issue in many states like Rhode Island, where the health insurance market is dominated by a near-monopoly between Blue Cross Blue Shield and United Healthcare.

Senator Michael Enzi of Wyoming introduced just such a bill in Congress, called the Health Insurance Marketplace Modernization and Affordability Act. This bill would have allowed small businesses to join together and create association health plans across state lines. Unfortunately, our esteemed leaders in the U.S. Senate, Chafee included, voted to filibuster the bill, keeping big insurance companies happy, the political contributions rolling in, and health insurance costs outrageously high.

The fundamental difference between Republicans and Democrats is that Republicans think people are smart and capable of making their own decisions. Democrats believe people need a babysitter in the form of the federal government. The economy, though, is a complicated beast and no one—not even the government—can predict the thousandth move of an intricate world economy. No one understood this lesson better than Mickey Rourke, who told William Hurt in the 1981 film *Body Heat*, "Are you ready to hear something? I want you to see if this sounds familiar: anytime you try a decent crime, you got fifty ways you're gonna *$%! up. If you think of twenty-five of them, then you're a genius ... and you ain't no genius." The same could be said for the federal government.

In the end, government is incapable of offering solutions that uniquely fit people's individual needs and desires. All it can offer are clunky, one-size-fits-all solutions. The Health Care Freedom Plan, while not the total solution to the country's health care ills, opens up the marketplace for people to take control of their own lives and make the decisions that best suit their needs. It is the government's way of saying, "We trust you. We trust America."

PORK–PUT AMERICA FIRST

The solution to cutting pork-barrel spending is not a difficult one. It is simply to cut it. The difficulty lies in its implementation, for the simple reason that asking Congress to cut pork is a bit like giving a band of criminals a stash of guns and asking them to police themselves. That said, there are a number of good proposals that would go a long way toward helping Congress wean itself off of its pork addiction.

During my race, I proposed a solution that would require a separate vote on each earmark and a two-thirds majority in order to attach any earmark to a bill. Similar legislation was introduced by a bipartisan group of senators in February 2006, called the Pork-Barrel Reduction Act, allowing senators to object to specific earmarks without the need to vote against the entire bill. Unless there are sixty votes in favor of the earmark, the objection will stand. Other important provisions require all earmarks to be listed in the bill text, conference reports to be filed and publicly available for at least forty-eight hours before floor consideration, and full disclosure on any earmarks, including the identity of the lawmaker seeking the earmark. Despite the bill's bipartisan support, there is a better chance of Dennis Kucinich cinching the Democratic presidential nomination than the bill seeing the light of the Senate floor anytime soon.

Short of new legislation and an unprecedented wave of self-control on the part of Congressional leaders, the war against pork-barrel spending must start at the top. As the leader of the country and the Republican Party, it is the president's job to say, "the buck stops here," and whip out his veto pen. Although Bush spent six years ignoring this problem, there is recent cause for optimism, albeit cautious optimism. In a Saturday radio address shortly after the midterm elections, President Bush urged Congress to push forward with earmark reform:

When you decide how to spend your paycheck, you have to set priorities and live within your means. Congress needs to do the same thing with the money you send to Washington. That was one of the clear messages American voters sent in the midterm elections. And one of the best ways we can impose more discipline on federal spending is by addressing the problem of earmarks.

These are encouraging words to be sure, but Republicans have long campaigned against wasteful spending and an increasingly large federal government. It is not enough to talk about cutting wasteful spending; they actually have to do it. If President Bush is truly interested in turning over a new leaf, he'd do himself a favor to heed the advice of a well-intentioned post to the National Review Online's blog called Sixers (http://sixers.nationalreview.com). It doesn't get much simpler than this:

White House to do list

[Greg Pollowitz 11/08 12:34 AM]

1. FIND veto stamp

2. BUY ink for veto stamp

3. ASK Alberto how Executive Privilege works again

IMMIGRATION–SECURE THE BORDER

The only way to curtail illegal immigration is to start at the root of the problem. This means, first and foremost, securing the border. A combination of fences, infrared cameras, and more border patrol agents will go a long way to alleviating the problem. Congress just needs to actually do it; otherwise, we will be having the same conversation twenty years from now, but instead of talking about twelve million illegal aliens, we'll be talking about twenty-five million.

Second, we need to enforce our policies currently in place against employers who hire illegal immigrants. In 1986, the Immigration Reform and Control Act empowered the Immigration and Naturalization Service to penalize companies that hire illegal immigrants. Unfortunately, this power has not been used and our laws have not been enforced. From 1997 to 2003, the number of investigations targeting employers of illegal aliens fell by more than 70 percent, from 7,637 to 2,194. During the same time, arrests on job sites fell from 17,554 to 445 and fines levied for immigration violations fell from 778 to 124.

With a zero-tolerance policy in place, illegal aliens will return home for the simple reason that employers will be too afraid to hire them. Once again, the solution to the problem lies in the most basic of economic principles: if you take away the incentive to stay, people will leave.

As an important side note, Republicans should not fall prey to the worst-case scenario that liberals like to toss out on the Sunday-morning talk shows—the man who came here twenty-five years ago, opened a pizza shop, put his kid through Harvard, and just didn't fill out his papers right. To be sure, there are a small group of heart-wrenching stories, and these folks should be able to apply for exceptions on an individual case basis. But the debate about illegal immigration in this country is not about the extreme example; it is about what is best for America and its citizens.

Once a firm enforcement program is in place, we can decide on the size of our guest worker program in accordance with the country's economic needs. If we really need twenty-five thousand people picking strawberries in California, so be it. Let the strawberry growers of California organize people at the border in conjunction with the federal government, document these workers, test them for diseases, give them forge-proof identification cards, and transport them safely to their destination. In order to ensure that workers return home after their allotted time expires, employers will deposit an additional sum of money into a fund at the border that the workers will receive on their way home. This guest worker program, however, has nothing to do with immigration and a path to citizenship, and it is important that the debate in this country does not confuse the two. The economic needs of this country can be fulfilled without succumbing to destructive amnesty programs.

Finally, all these policies will promote economic growth south of the border by forcing Mexico and its neighbors to deal with the problems that they have avoided for the last one hundred years, such as lack of competition in the energy industry, a lousy tax-collection system, and inflexible labor laws.[4] A stable and secure U.S.-Mexico border is exactly the kind of impetus Mexico needs to make the transition from a third world country to a first. Some activists in Mexico even hail the border as an opportunity that will force Mexico to deal with the real problem: the lack of economic growth that keeps people from staying in Mexico. Mexican activist Primitivo Rodriguez told the *New York Times* in May 2006: "[The wall is] the best thing that could happen for migrants, and for Mexico … If Mexicans were really shut inside their country, Mexico might be forced to get its own house in order."

WINNING THE WAR ON TERROR– TAKE THAT, ISLAMOFASCISTS

There has been a lot of talk about how to win the war on terror, and this is not the place for a lengthy treatise on foreign policy, but there is one significant area in which the Republican Party and President Bush have failed the American people, and it deserves mentioning. While there hasn't been a singular body blow, Republicans need to understand that we will not win the war on terror until we permanently drive the price of oil down to $15 a barrel.

There is really only one way to do that, and it's not ethanol. While I love the midwestern farmers dearly, they will never be able to grow enough corn or switchgrass to send the mullahs a message.

The best way to win any war is to keep our enemies from having the money to fight. We need to cut them off at the knees. But we can't do that as long as over 50 percent of our oil comes from foreign sources. Every time a barrel of oil goes up a dollar, that's another dollar Iranian president Mahmoud Ahmadinejad funnels to terrorist groups like Hezbollah and Hamas. Every time a gallon of gasoline tops $3, that's money Venezuelan president Hugo Chavez uses to jail another dissident.

We can increase our domestic oil supply, and we should. We should drill for more oil in the Gulf of Mexico and other oil-rich areas. But ultimately our energy needs are simply too big to be satisfied by our limited domestic supply. And nobody—except Jimmy Carter—should have to put on extra sweaters to stay warm in the winter. That's not the American way. The American way is to use market forces to develop new technologies and new sources of energy, such as major tax credits for producers and consumers of alternative energy sources like solar and wind power. What we need is a new national energy plan that gets us off foreign oil to win the war on terror, the likes of building the interstate highway system and putting a man on the moon.

When President Dwight D. Eisenhower introduced the National Interstate and Defense Highways Act of 1956, he did it for national security reasons. Fresh off of World War II, Eisenhower believed that a nationally synchronized highway system would allow the United States to transport its troops and resources at an optimum speed in case of another war. Imagine that Ohio ended its highway in the northern part of the state, but Indiana's highway picked up at the southern end—what a nightmare transportation would be. In peacetime this would be a traffic disaster, but in wartime the lack of coordination would spell imminent defeat.

The same is true of a decentralized energy plan. Already, individual states are devising their own plans to reduce our dependency on foreign oil. While Republicans tend to be small-government, leave-it-to-the-states kind of people, this has never been true when it comes to national security and defeating our enemies. While the Democrats need to realize that winning the war on terror is more important than saving that extra tree, Republicans need to admit that weaning the country off foreign oil is an integral part of this war.[5]

A HISTORY LESSON

Throughout the campaign, reporters asked Chafee why he remained a Republican when he agreed with Democrats on almost every issue. In response, Chafee spoke rhapsodically about the tradition of northeastern moderates and lamented the rise and influence of southern conservatives in the party. Often, he ended his stream of consciousness with a prayerful hope that the pendulum would swing back toward those good old moderate days.

This answer was peculiar for more than one reason, the relevant one being Chafee's shoddy memory of modern political history. Over the past fifty years, the Republican Party has witnessed one major success, and his name was Ronald Reagan. The Nelson Rockefellers and Gerald Fords of the Republican Party were a disaster, not only plunging the party into dissolution but also bringing the country down with it. The liberal wing of the Republican Party was responsible for, among other things, the Helsinki Accords, Supreme Court Justice John Paul Stevens, and Whip Inflation Now.

The Republican Party that Chafee speaks so fondly of was on the verge of extinction in 1974. With only 18 percent of the electorate identifying themselves as Republican, the party suffered greatly at the polls, losing forty-three seats in the House and four in the Senate, knocking its Senate population down to a dismal thirty-eight.

Writing in *Reagan's Revolution*, author Craig Shirley describes the Republican Party in the summer of 1974 as "bereft, bedraggled, unloved, and unwanted . . . If the GOP had been a stray cat, it would have been hauled away to the animal shelter and immediately euthanized—no one would have claimed it." Reporters and columnists predicted the party's impending death, going the way of the Whig Party in the 1850s. As the 1976 elections approached, things were so bad that there was talk of forming a third party with Reagan at the helm.

As the Republican Party of the 1970s struggled to hold on for dear life, the mainstream consensus was that the party needed to embrace its liberals, not reject them. When Reagan sprang onto the national stage challenging Ford for the nomination, the press scoffed at his chances and the wisdom of a turn to the right on the part of the GOP.

In 1976, *The New York Times* warned against an attempt at a right-wing revolution, "bloviating" that Reagan would destroy the Republican Party if he was nominated at the convention in Kansas City the following month. Calling him "an extremist" and citing his "wild positions" it warned that his nomination would result in the Republican Party going the way of "Bourbon kings." (Maybe this is when Rupert Murdoch thought up the "fair and balanced" approach he would later use at Fox News.)

In March 1975, *Newsweek* reported that the Republican establishment made its moderate preferences known, quickly lining up behind Ford and disseminating the equivalent of a pledge of allegiance. to members of Congress. In the next three days, the pledge was signed by over 75 percent of Republican members of the House and Senate. Hindsight, though, is a wonderful thing. Thirty years after the know-it-alls dismissed Reagan and his right-wing followers as a passing phase or, worse, the party's death knell, it was Reagan who brought the party back from the dead. It was Reagan who created a party viable of taking control of the Senate in 1980 and both houses of Congress in 1994—the first time the Republicans took control of the House in forty years. In a 2004 *Time* magazine article, reporters Nancy Gibbs and Matthew Cooper wrote, "We know a legacy when we see one. Ronald Reagan not only changed the landscape when he was in office, but had also fundamentally changed his party."

Following the Republican thumping in the 2006 election cycle, Senator Chuck Schumer announced that "Reaganomics is dead . . . the Reagan philosophy is dead." Simon Rosenberg, president of the New Democratic Network, chimed in with his partisan analysis: "Despite the many billions spent in building this modern conservative movement, history will label it a grand and remarkable failure. And we will look back at 2006 as the year this most recent period of American history—the conservative ascendancy—ended." Wishful thinking, but far from the truth.

Schumer, Simon Rosenberg, and their liberal friends do not even realize the extent to which Reaganism has permeated the political climate. Once upon a time, the conservative wing of the Republican Party was viewed as a bunch of pariahs. Today, no serious presidential candidate can make a credible run for the nomination without its support. Once upon a time, the notion that tax cuts created economic growth was ridiculed as "voodoo economics." Today, a whopping 61 percent of Americans and 51 percent of Democrats think tax hikes hurt the economy, according to a Rasmussen poll. Reagan didn't just win the presidency, he changed the very nature of the party and the very nature of the debate in this country. He took the invisible hand of Adam Smith out of the world of policy wonks and reintroduced it in basic and simple terms (with the help of Milton Friedman) to Americans across the ideological spectrum.

More recently, when oil hit $70 a barrel in the summer of 2006, no one spoke about reviving the odd-even license plates program of the 1970s. Thanks to Reagan, the economic theory of rationing has gone the way of buggy whips. And while there remain some economic doofuses spouting about a windfall profits tax on oil companies, Reagan's legacy has effectively removed the idea from the realm of serious policy proposals and relegated it to the domain of left-wing buffoonery.

Contrary to Chuck Schumer's predictions, Reaganism is alive and well, and proof that the only way back to power is the way Republicans got there in the first place. The press uses the word "moderate" like it's a magical token and mumbles the word "conservative" like it's a four-letter word, but Republicans never did better than when they were proud of who they were, and never did worse than when they pretended to be something they weren't. When Reagan was questioned by reporters about statements claiming he was too extreme, he responded, according to Shirley, unabashedly: "I think moderation should be taken in moderation . . . When you're on the operating table, you hope the doctor has more than just moderate skills. Let's put what we and our party believe on our banner and not water it down."

Over the past six years the Republican Party sacrificed one too many principles in the name of getting elected. If there is one lesson to be learned from the 2006 election cycle, it is that sacrificing our principles is a recipe for defeat. The next time our party leaders are faced with a choice of backing a senator like Linc Chafee or instituting a new federal entitlement program, they need to ask, as *Newsweek* reported, the same question Reagan asked a crowd of Republicans in 1975: "No one can quarrel with the idea that a political party hopes it can attract a wide following, but does it do this by forsaking its basic beliefs? By blurring its image so as to be indistinguishable from the opposition party?" The crowd answered these questions decisively: "No, no, no."

As we look at the Republican Party today and its high and low points over the past thirty years, we should take hope in knowing that we are not wandering alone in the desert without a plan or a platform. We already have a blueprint for success. But first we have to stop repeating the mistakes of the past.

You've read a lot in this book about the choices the Republican Party faced between principle and power. The epitome of this choice was when the national Republicans embraced Lincoln Chafee and attacked a Reagan Republican like myself. It was the case when they lined up like lemmings behind No Child Left Behind. It was the case when they said, "Forget the Contract with America and bring home the bacon." These choices are inherent to the political process, and they will never end. We will always be forced to choose between our principles and the short-term gains of bucking those principles.

I say: Damn the torpedoes and go with principle.

Notes

INTRODUCTION

1. Rhode Island's only state prison is located in Cranston.

2. This nickname was given to Chafee by local radio host Dan Yorke because of the inordinate amount of time Chafee spent at his Virginia home.

CHAPTER 1

1. According to the *Providence Journal*, Chafee explained that his vote didn't count because "the state is expected to vote overwhelmingly for Democrat John F. Kerry." Later on in the day, however, Chafee said that "he did not mean to imply that his vote would not count: 'If I did say yes, I regret that. I think I was more moving on to the next question.' "

2. Senator Jim Jeffords of Vermont abandoned the Republican Party in May 2001, becoming an Independent and caucusing with the Democrats, thereby giving the Democrats the slimmest of majorities in the Senate.

3. Running on a platform of eliminating the position and spending no money, the Cool Moose candidate for lieutenant governor, Bob Healey, actually got over 13 percent of the vote.

CHAPTER 2

1. In reality, Senator Chafee played no role in starting my career. Chafee enjoyed peddling this line throughout the campaign, but its relationship to the truth is nil. I met with Senator Chafee (and many others) before I decided to run for mayor in 2001. Chafee told me how much he enjoyed being the mayor of Warwick, but ultimately my decision to run for mayor of Cranston was based on my own desire to help the city that raised me and the encouragement of my friends and family, neither of which included Lincoln Chafee. As I pointed out to Chafee during our second radio debate, "Senator, you played no role in my decision process. I don't mean that in a rude way. I'm trying to be very polite. I didn't know you, and so when I meet with people I don't know, I don't tip my hand at what I'm going to do."

2. Yes, Chafee actually worked illegally shoeing horses in Canada. In a speech before the Harness Racing Congress in February 2002, Chafee spoke glowingly of his horse days in Canada: "I got to the border in Montana, went to the old shoeing school to say hi to Scott my old teacher. He said, 'I don't think you can make it across the border. They're not going to let you across the border.' I kind of hid my tools in the back of the trunk, and luckily when I crossed the border they didn't open my trunk, or I think they would have turned me around."

3. This point was driven home rather sharply when Chafee announced two days after losing the general election that he was considering leaving the party for good. More on this in Chapter 9.

4. When Chafee voted against drilling in the Arctic National Wildlife Refuge, he did so because he was concerned about a grizzly bear named Toby. In a December 23, 2005, *Providence Journal* article, environmental writer Peter Lord reported that Chafee stood up on the Senate floor and recounted the following story about his trip to Alaska: "Three years ago, he and his wife, Stephanie Chafee, had an opportunity to fly over the Brooks Range in the refuge, and camp for three days. They saw grizzly bears every day. They saw ptarmigan. They missed the caribou herd, which migrates north through the mountains each year so the females can give birth to their calves on the coastal plain. But they did see one old bull. Then, they visited Prudhoe Bay, where they stayed at a hotel that is basically a series of steel boxes, linked together. Chafee said the clerk at the hotel warned them about a bear named Toby that was roaming around outside the hotel. 'You don't want to surprise him,' the clerk said. A few months later, Chafee said, he read a story in a newspaper saying that Toby had to be shot. He had broken into the hotel, and had been wandering the halls, looking for food. During a Senate battle several months later, Chafee said Toby's plight explained why it was necessary to have an Arctic National Wildlife Refuge."

CHAPTER 3

1. Soloveichiks are a Rabbinic dynasty going back to the nineteenth century whose influence in Europe, Israel, and America is well-known among Jews. When Solly sent us her résumé, Zisserson and Mr. X—both Jewish—oohed and ahhed over her last name. "This is great, Mayor," they told me. "This is really great."

CHAPTER 4

1. In a January 2006 article for *Roll Call*, political analyst Stu Rothenberg proposed "that the Republicans send Rhode Island Sen. Lincoln Chafee to the Democrats in return for Nebraska Sen. Ben Nelson," as an "old-fashioned one-for-one deal. Rocky Colavito for Harvey Kuenn. Let's get totally real about what's going on here. Chafee is a Democrat, and Nelson is a Republican. They just find themselves trapped in the wrong parties. It's like one of those 'Freaky Friday' movies."

2. Visiting Rhode Island for his second Chafee fund-raiser in early October 2006, McCain declared: "I am a conservative Republican. I repeat: I am a conservative Republican."

3. More than a year later, as this manuscript goes to press, I still haven't heard from the FEC. No doubt, they had more important things to worry about.

CHAPTER 5

1. The NRSC sent out a mailer claiming, "Steve Laffey wanted the taxpayers to buy a new vehicle for him when he became mayor. But the city said they couldn't afford one due to the budget crisis, especially a luxury SUV . . . His new vehicle of choice: a black 2004 Mercury Mountaineer equipped with a tan leather interior. Apparently, a regular interior isn't good enough for Steve Laffey." The truth (if you actually care): The previous mayor had two cars, which I thought was ridiculous. When I became mayor, the city went out to bid for *one* car with *cloth* seats, and the winning bid—50 percent less than the cost of the previous mayor's car—happened to come with a leather interior.

2. I still don't understand why the local grocery store sold six dozen eggs to six kids on Halloween night. That's an awful lot of eggs for some "pancake batter."

3. Ironically, Senator Chafee supported Jackvony in the primary, sending out a letter of support to his constituents, even though he wasn't the endorsed candidate.

4. In our first radio debate, Senator Chafee argued regarding the conflict between Israel and Hezbollah in Lebanon, that "a bad peace is better than a good war." When I heard this statement, I immediately thought of Chamberlain's infamous "Peace in Our Time" speech.

5. During Condoleezza Rice's confirmation hearings for secretary of state, Chafee asked Rice whether there was potential to find common ground with Iran. He recommended that the United States look at "the success we had with the thaw with the People's Republic of China [that] had a lot to do with the exchange of ping-pong teams, of all things." Kudos to Condoleezza Rice for keeping a straight face.

6. On the campaign trail, I met hordes of journalists from all over the country and even some from other parts of the world. For the record, there were plenty of reporters who did an excellent job, regardless of their political ideology. Kudos to all of you. You make America a better place.

CHAPTER 6

1. "GOP Forced to Fight for Rebel Chafee: His Challenger in the Primary May Be Too Conservative to Win R.I.," *Washington Post*, September 10, 2006.

2. In 2004, Planned Parenthood introduced a new addition to its online store: fitted tees with the words "I Had an Abortion," stamped front and center across the fabric. According to the Planned Parenthood Web site, "These soft and comfortable tees assert a powerful message in support of women's rights."

CHAPTER 7

1. *Red Dawn* was a 1984 cult classic set in the small town of Calumet, Colorado, bombarded by a Soviet invasion. A group of teenagers from the local high school, calling themselves the Wolverines after their school mascot, bravely take on the occupying Soviet forces. Famous eighties stars Patrick Swayze, Charlie Sheen, Lea Thompson, and Jennifer Grey starred in the film.

2. From *Merriam-Webster's Collegiate Dictionary* (eleventh edition): [G, fr. *Schaden* damage + *Freude* joy] (1895): enjoyment obtained from the troubles of others.

3. Unprincipled.

4. Debates now! Beep beep!

CHAPTER 8

1. Being the strategic thinker that I was, I declared the bathroom "out of order." At the end of the day, somebody had to empty out the tank—in RV parlance, the "black water"—and I had a suspicious feeling it was going to be me. The "out of order" bathroom became something of a legend. Before the second debate, host Dan Yorke asked my ten-year-old son, Sam, on live radio whether the bathroom was truly off limits. Without missing a beat, Sam replied: "Uh, it's off limits to everyone except my little sister Audrey and . . . and Harry the Greek, our driver."

2. On September 23, 2004, Chafee was one of only three U.S. senators to vote against maintaining middle-class tax relief that had cut taxes by $1,800 for a family of four making $35,000 a year.

3. Caserta may be the gold standard in Rhode Island, but the Laffey campaign and its volunteers subsisted on the pizza from The Big Cheese, Campanella's Restaurant, and Superior Bakery. Thanks, everyone.

4. Hamantaschen are triangular cookies with jelly fillings that Jews eat on the Jewish festival of Purim.

CHAPTER 9

1. The Democratic primary for the U.S. Senate in Rhode Island effectively ended when Secretary of State Matt Brown dropped out of the race after an early spending spree on television ads and a fund-raising scandal. No doubt, this helped Chafee's get-out-the-liberal-vote effort.

2. On September 13, 2006, John Miller of the *National Review* posted the following on the NRO blog called The Corner: "For what it's worth, when I contacted the Chafee campaign a couple of months ago to see if Chafee would support a victorious, GOP-nominated Laffey in the general election, the answer was not 'yes.' "

3. In the 2002 Republican gubernatorial primary, the *total* number of votes cast was less than twenty-six thousand, about average for a Rhode Island Republican primary.

4. At the same press conference, Chafee admitted as much, saying, "I'm proud that I was able to deliver for Rhode Island by being a member of the majority party—that was a big part of uh, uh, my position why I stayed . . . Jim Jeffords—he jumped in '01, I was pretty much brand new there, he'd been there for, uh, I think since the early seventies, he came in in Watergate, and once he did that there was no real need to anymore; it wouldn't have

changed anything to look at my options, and I wanted to look out for Rhode Island . . . The highway bill is important."

CHAPTER 10

1. Representative David Obey (D-WI) secured federal funds for a wind-powered ice sled for the sheriff of Ashland County, Wisconsin.

2. For example, a 1998 Harvard study found that students participating in the Milwaukee voucher program gained eleven points in math and six points in reading, while a study by Cecilia Rouse of Princeton in the same year found voucher students "outperformed the control group by eight points in math over four years." A study in 2004 found that the graduation rate in 2003 for those participating in the voucher program was 64 percent, compared with a graduation rate of 36 percent for those in Milwaukee's public schools.

3. A 2003 Phi Delta Kappa/Gallup poll found that 62 percent of Americans favor tuition voucher programs. According to a 2002 poll by the Joint Center for Political and Economic Study, 74 percent of black households with children and 57 percent of blacks support voucher programs. The same poll found that 66.8 percent of Hispanic households with children supported vouchers.

4. In February 2005, I traveled with Rhode Island's Latino leaders across the Arizona border into Altar, Mexico, and saw firsthand the corruption, the plight of the illegal immigrants, and the turmoil caused by the massive influx of workers out of Mexico and onto American soil.

5. Secondary benefits of a new national energy plan, while subservient to winning the war on terror, are substantial in their own right. These include more American manufacturing jobs that are currently going overseas in the solar and wind industry, a healthier environment, leapfrogging over Democrats on the issue of global warming, and muting our allies in Old Europe.

Index

Page numbers in italics refer to illustrations.

elections, congressional:
  of 1974, 191–92
  of 1994, 7, 18, 163, 164, 173, 193
  of 2000, 54–55
  of 2006, 12, 18, 37, 43, 100, 153,
    155–62, 163–65, 167, 172,
    179, 193, 194
elections, presidential:
  of 1884, 97
  of 1964, 78
  of 1976, 98–99
  of 1980, 168, 193
  of 1984, 109, 110
  of 1996, 168
  of 2000, 168
  of 2004, 70, 172
  of 2008, 71, 72
Elementary and Secondary
  Education Act (No Child Left
  Behind) (2002), 7, 155, 160,
  165, 169–71, 177, 195
energy policy, 39, 179, 189–91,
  198*n*, 202*n*
Erdogan, Recep Tayyip, 88
ethanol, 190

Federal Election Commission
  (FEC), 13
  NRSC complaint against Laffey
    filed with, 73–77, 199*n*
Feingold, Russ, 68, 99
Feinstein, Diane, 177
Field of Dreams, 50
File This with Phil Anez, 115
Ford, Gerald R., 47, 98–99, 158, 165,
  191, 192
Ford, Harold, Jr., 37, 108, 161, 165
Forward, 89
Fox News, 136
Fred (campaign adviser), 57–58,
  153–54
Fred Sanford, 118
Free to Choose (Friedman), 183
Free to Choose (television series), 3
free trade issue, 45

Friedman, Milton, 2, 3, 56, 180, 183,
  194
Frist, Bill, 70
Fung, Allan, *85*

gay marriage issue, 131, 165
General Electric, 110–11
George (campaign staffer), 54–55,
  130
Gibbs, Nancy, 193
Gingrich, Newt, 163, 164
Glover, Helen, 120
Goldwater, Barry S., 78
Gore, Al, 182
Government Accountability Office
  (GAO), 170
Graham, Lindsey, 70
Gregg, Judd, 169
Gregory, David, 89
Grey, Jennifer, 200*n*

hamantaschen, 142, 201*n*
Hamas, 89, 190
Happy Days, 119
Harkin, Tom, 175
Harness Racing Congress, 198*n*
Harry the Greek (campaign staffer),
  52–54, 130, 133, 137, 138–39,
  201*n*
Harvard Business School, 3, 4,
  22–23
Harvard University, 170
Hawaii, pork-barrel spending for,
  174
Hazelwood, Blaise, 151
Healey, Bob, 197*n*
health care, 165, 166, 171–72,
  182–85
Health Care Freedom Plan, 183–85
health insurance, 184–85
Health Insurance Marketplace
  Modernization and
  Affordability Act, 185
health savings accounts (HSAs),
  183–84